"One of the truly great teachers of theology in the second half of the 20th century, Bernard Cooke has been instructing and inspiring students for more than forty years. Those who have heard him lecture have been in awe of the depth and clarity that characterize his presentations. In *Why Angels?* he provocatively presents his reflections on angels in relation to other Christian mysteries. Readers of this book, even if they disagree with his theological reasoning, will be moved to reflect on their own faith and decide which Christian mysteries are central to their own spirituality."

Rev. Robert E. Lauder
St. John's University

"It takes courage these days to write another book on angels. But this one is worth it. Cooke's insights on why we believe in guardian angels strike a wonderful tone of respect for this tradition in Christian spirituality, and at the same time demonstrate how that belief connects to a deeper awareness of Christ's intimacy with us, and of our sacramental presence to one another in the Communion of Saints."

Rev. John Dietzen
Pastor, *Catholic News Service* Columnist

"This is a thought-provoking commentary on the role of angels in the Bible, tradition, and contemporary experience. Cooke raises an important question: if people were to experience God's Spirit in their lives more powerfully, would angels be so popular today? Cooke emphasizes the ministry of the baptized. All of us are meant to be 'guardian angels to one another' in the discipleship of equals."

Bridget Mary Meehan,
Author, *Praying With Passionate Women*

"There are probably more angel books out lately than one could stack on the head of a pin. Most, sadly, have less substance than an angel's feathers. Bernard Cooke's angels are part of his awareness of life. They do not come and go like pizza delivery boys. They are symbols of God's unbroken attention to us. In Cooke's words, they are an 'implicit message of God's presence.'"

Tim Unsworth
National Catholic Reporter

"Drawing on his broad knowledge of the concept of sacramentality, Cooke carefully uncovers the culturally-conditioned view of angels as God's messengers and advocates. He argues that such a perspective can and should give way to the contemporary Christian awareness of God's personal presence in each of us through the power of the Holy Spirit. Because we are all sacraments to one another, our guardian angel may well be the spouse, parent, or friend right next to us.

"Angel lovers, beware! This brief angelic journey may bring you face to face not with an angel, but with the risen presence of Christ himself. And before you 'fly off the handle' you should take time to find out where those wings really came from: God's revelation . . . or Persia!

Edmond J. Dunn
Theology Chair, St. Ambrose University

"Bernard Cooke raises important questions about belief in angels and their current popularity. After reading this book both those who take angels seriously and those who do not will be better informed about what they do or do not believe. *Why Angels?* is a delightful conversation with a top theologian on many key issues of Christian faith."

Mitch & Kathy Finley,
Authors, *Building Christian Families*

"In the midst of all the commercialization of angels comes Bernard Cooke's incisive, warm book inviting us to take a serious look at our beliefs about angels. He gives an impressive synthesis of the biblical and historical background of angelology and raises important questions about the place of angels in contemporary spirituality. He shows that belief in angels developed out of dualistic theology that separated body and spirit, and out of a hierarchical world view that placed angels in the gap between earth and heaven. A true understanding of Jesus living within us eliminates this gap.

Jann Aldredge-Clanton
Baylor University Medical Center
Author, *In Search of the Christ-Sophia*

BERNARD COOKE

WHY *Angels?*

Are They Real...
Really Needed?!

TWENTY-THIRD PUBLICATIONS
Mystic, CT 06355

Twenty-Third Publications
185 Willow Street
P.O. Box 180
Mystic, CT 06355
(860) 536-2611
800-321-0411

ISBN 0-89622-686-7
Library of Congress Catalog Card Number 95-62068
Printed in the U.S.A.

Contents

Introduction   1

Chapter One
Early Teaching about Angels   7
- The Loss of Spirit
- Do Angels Exist?
- Manifestations of God
- The Prophetic Tradition
- The "Divine" Sun
- New Testament Angels
- Who Did Jesus Send?
- The Teaching of St. Bernard
- What Augustine Taught

Chapter Two
Understanding God's Presence   23
- An Army of God's Angels
- Blessed Beyond Measure
- God Communicates With Us
- A Sense of the Divine Presence
- Rediscovering the Presence of Christ
- What Happened to Guardian Angels?
- A Discipleship of Equals

Chapter Three

We Share God's "Spirit Power"   39

  • Harnessing God's Spirit
  • How We Experience the Spirit
  • A Sign of God's Concern
  • Is God's Action Extraordinary?
  • God's Spirit in Creation
  • We Share a Great Gift

Chapter Four

We Are All Sacraments of God   51

  • Creatures of Space and Time
  • Looking for Deeper Meaning
  • A Negative Influence
  • God's Presence Is Reality
  • Spiritual Separated from Bodily
  • Second-Class Status in the Church
  • Appreciating the Ordinary
  • Community With Heavenly Friends

Chapter Five

We Are a Communion of Saints   63

- •Angels Were in Charge
- •Challenging Favored Beliefs
- •Belief in the Afterlife
- •Bonds Between Living and Dead
- •Christ Is Still Active

Chapter Six

Lingering Questions About Angels   73

- •Should Belief in Angels Be Discouraged?
- •What Should We Teach?
- •Why Emphasize Saints and Not Angels?
- •What Does the Church Teach?
- •Are There Really Choirs of Angels?
- •Why Did Jesus Refer to Angels?
- •What Should Homilists Preach?
- •What about Angelic "Experiences"?
- •Are There Really "Fallen Angels"?

Continuing the Discussion   83

I can understand why people of my
generation would hold on to their childhood
beliefs about angels, but why are so many
young people today interested in angels?

Introduction

One of the remarkable cultural developments in recent years in the United States is the resurgence of interest in angels. Despite the demythologizing of so many things religious, which resulted from the exaltation of science and especially of psychology, there is widespread interest and belief in beings who are superior to humans and yet deeply implicated in human affairs.

Perhaps it is part of people being fascinated by the possibility of extra-terrestrials, of flying saucers, of visitors or invaders from other planets. But that doesn't seem to be the explanation; angels are thought of and imagined by people as quite different from these other-planetary beings; angels are not from other planets but from "heaven" wherever that is. However they are imagined, angels are everywhere these days: Books about them abound in bookstores, Christmas trees are hung with them, hundreds of little statuettes of cherubs remind residents of Los Angeles that they do indeed inhabit the city of the angels. Angels are definitely in.

Of course, for one of my vintage, growing up in the "naive" Catholicism of the pre-Vatican era, angels were taken for granted. Among the prayers we learned in early childhood there was always "Angel of God, my guardian dear...." And as we grew into adolescence, if earlier beliefs still remained—and they generally did in those days—a guardian angel was more than once appealed to as an assistant in fighting off "temptation." We did have a balanced angelology: Along with the good angel who guarded us from the evil one, there was the evil one, a minor devil assigned, not to help us do good but to seduce us to sin.

One of the most fascinating pieces of popular literature I read years ago was C.S. Lewis' *The Screwtape Letters*. As many will recall, it was a small gem of a book, the first book of his that I had read and that hooked me forever on his writings. It pretended to be a collection of letters sent by a second-level devil to report to his superior back in hell the developments in the mission of leading his assigned human to perdition.

It was, really, a delightfully insightful description of the various psychological mechanisms by which we humans avoid responsibility in the midst of our all-too-frequent moral infidelity. *The Screwtape Letters* could have enjoyed the popularity it did only because there was still a widespread lurking belief that there actually existed such "bad angels." In much the same way, a generation later, Flip Wilson's comic remark, "The devil made me do it" resonated with people and was repeated again and again—not as a statement of fact, but reflecting our tendency to blame someone else. And it did suggest that there might just be such personal tempters stalking us.

Focus on the Devil

Then, too, a few decades back there was a rash of writing about "the devil"; did he or did he not exist? (Strangely, or perhaps not so strangely, the devil was always a "he," as were the "good angels"). Connected with this awakened interest in Satan were increased awareness of Satanic worship in certain circles, and almost compulsive interest in "diabolic possession." *The Exorcist*, first as a book and then as a movie, frightened a few million people at the same time as it attracted them with irresistible fascination. The suggestion that such things did actually happen, and a certain amount of "objective" evidence that they *had* happened, only reinforced the popular conviction that the devil was very real and still roamed the earth. I remember that on rainy dreary Friday afternoons, when classes were notoriously difficult to teach, nothing so did the trick as a discussion of diabolic possession. It worked even better than talking about sex.

More Than Enough Evil

The last couple of decades have focused less on "the evil one," perhaps because the daily TV reporting of human violence more than accounts for evildoing in the world. Instead, we have seen any number of books and newspaper features and movies about God-sent spirits, "good angels," appearing in human form to guide and even save humans in their moments of crisis. Quite regularly, around Christmas time, TV stations bring back the movie in which the character played by Jimmy Stewart, despondent because of a number of setbacks and threatened with economic disaster, is on the brink of committing suicide. But just as he is about to throw himself off a bridge a friendly apprentice angel, Clarence, intervenes to save him. In so doing, Clarence wins his wings as a certified guardian angel. Apparently that movie won a wide audience, for since its appearance any number of shows have revolved around an angel in human form who manages to save foolish humans despite themselves.

As a matter of fact, some of these shows have developed into full series in which angels in human form intervene week after week to help the needy. Interestingly, in these series the angels usually work in teams of two, probably because the dialogue between them is needed to make clear their heavenly identity. Whether such television productions reflect a real belief in angelic assistance, or whether they are just delightful fiction whose very unreality frees watchers from any serious reflection, they do seem to suggest that people are open to the idea of guardian angels and may actually have a sense that "someone up there" is watching over them through these intermediaries.

A Contemporary Drama

Just this week as I was writing this, there was a TV show about a rancorous baseball coach who mercilessly rides herd on his players, always being the tough guy. He is particularly rough on his star player, a kind and sensitive and athletically gifted young man who was raised without a father, and who looks up to the coach as a hero and father figure. Beneath the coach's harsh exterior lies the sad story of his own shattered dreams. He had been a talented baseball player and a local hero in high school, already destined for big league stardom when he was seriously injured and all but killed in Vietnam. As a result, his athletic career was cut short. He had been the town athletic legend when in high school, is still the town hero because his coaching has brought the local high school team to national eminence; but this coaching success has done nothing to overcome his bitterness.

Enter an angel, appearing (contrary to the ordinary pattern of "male" angels) in the form of an attractive young woman teacher who is asked to fill in as assistant coach because of an accident to the regular assistant. Needless to say, her appearance on the scene and her more kindly approach to the team members win no favor with the coach. However, she alone knows the deeper reason for the coach's present bitterness. He is near death from cancer, though he has successfully hidden his condition so that no one around him suspects. Totally unreconciled to this fate, he tries to hide it even from himself. His hostility turns even his star player against him and they become involved in a fight just before he collapses on the field and is rushed to the hospital.

All this happened on the eve before the big game. As he lies dying in the hospital, the assistant coach visits him and he realizes why she has seemed familiar to him. She is the same one who when he was dying on the battlefield in Vietnam came to him as a nurse and saved his life. She must be his angel. Through her bargaining with the angel of death, the coach is given an extra day. He uses it to reconcile himself with his young protégé, and he goes to the game to encourage his team as they win the state championship, after which his angel leads him into the life beyond. It does make for good drama!

One of the notable features of this interest in things angelic is its coincidence with "new age." It isn't too surprising to find books about angels in the bookstores of Catholic colleges, though I have been amazed at the large number on this topic, far more than on other topics that I consider central to Christian belief. Yet, go into into any "new age" bookstore or trinket store and you will find angel pendants, angel pictures, angel pins, even angel statuettes, competing for attention with crystals and exotic fragrances. And, of course, there are innumerable Christmas ornaments, angels of every size and shape.

One of the aspects of all this interest in angels really puzzles me. I can understand why people of my generation would want to preserve their attachment to angels as a somewhat nostalgic reminder of their childhood beliefs and practices. But why so many young people? Why angels? This is the question that prompts me to share the following reflections about angels with you. Why are young people, who are often (and I believe quite unjustly) referred to as the "me generation," so enthusiastic about angels? Somehow, for reasons that escape me, angels fit into the culture of crystals, "The Living Dead," and jeans.

The Greek word *aggelos* in the New
Testament simply means "messenger,"
and of itself says nothing about
winged creatures or purely spiritual persons.

Chapter One

EARLY TEACHING
ABOUT ANGELS

No question about it; angels are in! But why? One disturbing response to this question, a response that finds a certain amount of historical precedent, is that angels are in because God is out. Historians of Christian thought in the West tell us that the past couple hundred years have witnessed an unprecedented and growing phenomenon: For many people, especially educated people, there is a total absence of God in their awareness of reality. Some philosophers have expressed this by saying "God is dead." They are not claiming that a transcendent creator who previously existed has now gone out of existence; what they are saying is that for large numbers of people the existence or reality of God is totally irrelevant. It isn't even a question worth considering. God has vanished from their perception of reality.

There have always been atheists who deny the existence of God; and there are agnostics who tell us that there is no way of knowing if there is or is not a God. But these people are dealing with the God who was commonly considered to exist, a God whose being or non-being is something of ultimate importance. Even David Hume, the eighteenth-century philosopher who argued so tellingly against the supposed "proofs" for God's existence, could never let go of the God-question. Like a dog with a bone, he grappled with the issue to the very end of his life. This is not, however, what is going on for so many of our contemporaries. For them the God-question is truly "dead and buried."

The Loss of Spirit

This leaves a void; it leaves no grounding for the final importance of "spirit." This is probably why a number of recent books have highlighted the failure of things material, the failure of our consumerist obsession with things, the failure of wondrous advances in comfort and entertainment, to fill this void. In the midst of this loss of the god-awareness, we humans are looking for something beyond what we are and can produce; we are looking for someone or something to provide some meaning that honors our reality as embodied spirits. Faced with the loss of "spirit" in our materialistic society, we cling to the notion that there is a world of spirits who, though superior to us, are still involved with us and somehow part of our world.

Perhaps, though, the opposite explanation is true: Perhaps the prominence of angels is a forecast of God's intensified presence to our history; perhaps before we humans can admit the awesome reality of divine presence we have to prepare for it by rumors of angels. Maybe, just maybe, angels are a sign of Advent before Christmas. But let me back up a bit before I propose that we are today on the brink of a new awareness of the presence of God, and let me say more about angels.

I must be honest. I grew up believing in my special guardian angel, and for years he (you'll notice it was a "he") was a companion and to some extent a conversation partner. At least I talked to him. But for a long time now, all that has ceased. Right now I feel no need at all for a guardian angel. Should I have one, I would certainly not object, I would never want to claim that I can continue profitably and safely on my life journey alone; and I would apologize to him for the neglect of recent years. Though there may be angels, even guardian angels, whose existence I certainly cannot deny, my candid reaction is: Why do we need them?

Do Angels Exist?

Before going on to explain why angels seem to me a bit superfluous, it would be only fair to hear the other side of the conversation, to say something about all the indications that angels do really exist and play a role in our lives. After all, there is a long, long history of humans believing in and trusting angels. It would be presumptuous and arrogant to dismiss that history as simply wrong and misguided, to assume that we in the twentieth century have suddenly become enlightened. Many of the greatest minds in Christianity, including Thomas Aquinas and Dante, whom I consider to be of unparalleled genius in Western history, have taken angels for granted. As a matter of fact, Aquinas bears the title "Angelic Doctor" precisely because of his magnificent description of the intellectual processes of these more-than-human personalities.

Long before Aquinas and Dante, in the sacred literature of Israel, there is mention of "angels" though scripture scholars tell us that we need to be careful not to impose later understandings on the biblical texts. Apparently, the term "the angel of the Lord" found early in Israel's literature, does not refer to a personage other than God. Rather, it seems that it is referring to God's own appearances to privileged humans.

This equation of an "angel of the Lord" with Yahweh is very clear in the scene where Abraham is about to sacrifice his son, Isaac. Just as Abraham raises the sacrificial knife, the angel of the Lord calls to him from heaven, "Abraham, Abraham." "I am here," he replies. "Do not raise your hand against the boy," the angel says. "Do not harm him, for now I know that you fear God. You have not refused me your son, your only son." The angel of Yahweh called a second time, "I swear by my own self—it is Yahweh who speaks—because you have done this, because you have not refused me your son, your only son, I will shower blessings on you" (Gen 22:11–18).

Later in the narrative of Israel's origins, when the people

were on the march out of Egypt and on their way to the desert, "the angel of the Lord" is identified with the cloud by day and fire by night that guided the wanderers and protected them from the enemy. "Then the angel of Yahweh, who marched in the front of the army of Israel, changed station and moved to their rear. The pillar of cloud changed station from the front to the rear of them, and remained there. It came between the camp of the Egyptians and the camp of Israel" (Ex 14:19).

There is a very interesting history of this cloud, symbol of God's protecting presence to the people. During the years of the desert wandering, according to the tradition recorded in Exodus, this cloud often came to rest at the entrance of the Tabernacle that housed the ark of the covenant. On such occasions Moses went there and spoke with God. This tent for the ark of the covenant, the Tabernacle, was seen by later generations as the forerunner of the Jerusalem Temple.

Manifestations of God

When the text of 1 Kings 8:10 describes the dedication of the Temple by Solomon, it says that the cloud, "the glory of Yahweh," filled the Temple as Yahweh took possession of it and made it the symbol of his constant presence with the chosen people. It would seem, then, that the term "the angel of Yahweh" refers in the Pentateuch to some manifestation of God's saving presence. Much the same can be said about the use of "the angel of Yahweh" as it occurs early in the book of Judges or in the story of Gideon's encounter with God.

Incidentally, it is always good to keep in mind that the Greek word *aggelos* in the New Testament (the word that a few centuries earlier the Septuagint, the Greek translation of the Hebrew bible, had used to translate the Hebrew *mal'ak*), simply means "a messenger," and of itself says nothing about winged creatures or purely spiritual persons.

There is some evidence that winged and individual angelic beings got into the picture and into popular Jewish religious belief quite late, only after the time of the people's exile in Babylon and

Persia. In the religion of the Persian part of the world there was belief in winged beings, both good and evil, who were more powerful than humans, and who influenced human life. Prior to that time, in the stories about Israel's origins and development there was some reference to superior beings other than God, beings like the seraphim and cherubim who surrounded the throne of God and formed part of God's glory, but who had little of what we would consider individual identity or involvement with human affairs. Every great king had to have a royal court, and so also Yahweh, the greatest of kings, had a heavenly court made up of seraphim and cherubim. It is only in late books of the bible, like Daniel and Tobias, that there is mention of angels with distinctive characteristics, with something like individual identity. However, as we will see, it is questionable if those passages are dealing with actual persons or with personifications of divine attributes.

The Prophetic Tradition

One of the most striking things about the bible's treatment of angels is the almost total lack of reference to angels in the prophetic writings that preceded the people's return from the Babylonian exile. The one isolated reference comes in the scene of Isaiah's prophetic vision, in which a seraph touches the prophet's tongue with a coal from the altar of incense. This absence assumes considerable importance when we realize that prophetic experience and the oracles that expressed it were the cutting edge of the process we call "revelation." And it was precisely the prophetic tradition that most influenced Jesus' Jewish understanding of the God he knew as his Abba.

Not surprising, then, that in his parables, where Jesus tried to explain how his Abba was working in people's lives, there is no mention of angels. Since in Israel's biblical texts there is no prominence of angels prior to the Persian period (roughly fourth and fifth centuries BCE), it seems plausible that angels, especially winged angels, are borrowed from Persian culture and do not directly or even indirectly come from "divine revelation."

But, how about Michael and Gabriel and Raphael? Isn't the bible quite explicit about their exploits? Michael led the heavenly armies as they drove Lucifer into unending punishment in hell. Gabriel bore God's various messages to humans, and Raphael guided God's chosen ones through the dangers of life. Again, without being too much a "doubting Thomas," it seems to me that responsible biblical scholarship suggests that Michael and company are "real," but that they are not "really archangels." That may sound like double-talk, but truly it isn't. You'll notice that each of those names ends with "el," which is the basic stem in Hebrew for "god" (e.g. in *Elohim*). So, very likely what we are dealing with are ways of naming various aspects of God in relation to humans: God's overcoming evil (Micha–el) or communicating with us (Gabri–el) or watching over and guiding us (Rapha–el). Such divine activity we may believe, is very real; but that need not mean that there are "real persons" who bear such names.

Personifying aspects of God or of the forces in nature was something the people of Israel shared with other ancient cultures. Humans have always been fascinated by and concerned about the order (or disorder) and power that they experience in nature or in human society. This is not primarily a matter of seeking a speculative understanding of the forces working around them; it is a matter of guaranteeing the forces that would benefit them and avoiding those that were destructive.

The "Divine" Sun

One of the clearest examples is the attitude of ancient peoples toward the sun, which most cultures saw as "divine." Obviously dependent upon the sun for light and warmth and the growth of crops, ancient people were always apprehensive at the approach of the winter solstice. Would the waning of sunlight be reversed or not? If not, humans were obviously in a great deal of trouble. So, religious rituals were performed to persuade, indeed to force, the sun god to once more lengthen the days. Such "divinizing" of the forces of the universe and in particular the force of life, was prominent in the cultures of the Mesopotamian valley and of Egypt (to which the chosen people were exposed in their origins) and in the Canaanite culture (into which they moved during the Exodus).

Israel, of course, in its later history moved toward monotheism and no longer worshiped a number of nature's forces as "gods." The Israelites saw their God, Yahweh, as creating and controlling all of human life and all of the happenings in the universe. So, instead of personifying elements of nature as "gods," the Israelites linked all of these elements to the power and action of Yahweh. Still the tendency to personify persisted. Some of the aspects of Yahweh's action on behalf of his people came to be personified, possibly as Michael or Gabriel or Raphael.

One such personification, that of divine Wisdom, has become the object of extensive study in recent years, particularly by women scholars who see great importance in the fact that divine Wisdom is a feminine personification. There is no claim that divine Wisdom is a being apart from God; rather, Wisdom is clearly God's wisdom, with God from eternity, present with God at the creation of the world, and imparted to humans in the process of Torah. Wisdom is not a person distinct from God, but rather it personifies the divine wisdom that God shares with the chosen people. In the theology of the New Testament, especially in the gospel of Luke, Jesus is seen to be the prophet, and even beyond that the embodiment of this divine wisdom.

New Testament Angels

In some ways the New Testament gospels seem to give more unassailable witness to the existence of angels, though not to their being winged beings. Luke's account of the message brought to Mary is basic to Christian belief about the unique parentage of Jesus, and what would that gospel scene be without Gabriel? How impoverished our art would be if there did not exist the Gabriels of Fra Angelico or of the great Flemish masters like Van Eyck. To clinch the argument: Jesus himself refers to angels on more than one occasion.

For example, when one of his disciples drew a sword to

defend him, Jesus reminded him, "Could I not ask and my Father would send ten legions of angels to defend me?" If one needed any more proof, there was the angel who after Jesus' resurrection came to Peter in prison and freed him from his captors. Yet, angels never show up in the parables that were the core of Jesus' teaching about God's activity in our lives. Some of these parables, like the one about the unjust custodians of the vineyard, do speak in symbol about messengers sent from God, but it is quite clear that they are references to the prophets of Israel; there are no hints that they might refer to angelic messengers.

Another thing that makes me wonder about Jesus' acceptance of and attitude towards guardian angels, is the account in the New Testament of Jesus' parting words to his close disciples. In the beautiful chapters of John's gospel that describe at length the Last Supper, Jesus speaks about his departure from them, at least in visible form, and he promises his friends that in some way he will always be with them.

Connected with this continuing presence, this abiding with them, is the promise of the Paraclete. There has always been dispute about the identity of this Paraclete. There is obviously a close connection with Christ's Spirit but will this Spirit take Jesus' place in history once the resurrection has occurred? One of the most carefully argued explanations given by scripture scholars today is that Christ, in the mystery of Easter and Pentecost, will remain present to his own in history through the communication of his and his Abba's Spirit, the Spirit of truth and life and love.

Who Did Jesus Send?

However, leaving aside this specific question, what I am trying to highlight here is that Jesus did not promise that guardian angels would watch over his disciples, would lead them to their destiny, would accompany them on their pilgrimage and help safeguard them from the temptations of "the world."

Much the same could be said of the "departure scenes" in the gospels of Luke and Matthew. Matthew's account in particular is very explicit about the continuing presence of Christ himself to his followers. "Behold, I am with you all days, even to the end of the world." None of these passages seem to indicate any need for guardian angels to replace Jesus' own guarding care for his disciples, unless, of course, people begin to lose the sense of Jesus' presence and begin to think of him as being far away, "up in heaven."

What conclusion can we draw from all this? For people of religious belief in ancient times, and there was little if any distinction between their cultural outlook and what might be called their religious belief, angels seem to have been part of their view of reality. It does seem that Jewish people of Jesus' day took angels for granted. Maybe the wings were imaginary, merely a symbol of angelic dwelling "in heaven above" or of the rapidity of angelic movement; but the more-than-human personages we call angels were not thought to be purely imaginary. People took for granted that they existed.

Still, in my efforts to accept the reality of angels and be reconverted to the beliefs of my younger years, I am faced with some basic and (at least for me) unresolved questions. Granted that many of Jesus' contemporaries, perhaps even Jesus himself, took angels for granted, was this because of their cultural worldview or because it was rooted in the religious traditions that grew out of Yahweh's revelations to the people over the centuries? It is one thing to agree with the Jewish belief that their God watched over them and guided their history; it is another to agree with the "scientific" view of the universe through which they interpreted that divine guidance. I am not sure whether angels belong to the revelation underlying their religious beliefs or to their cultural worldview.

In the history of early Christian belief, angels don't seem to be all that prominent, though there is some mention of them as taken for granted. They only started to assume importance when, in the wake of the Council of Nicaea and all the insistence on Christ's divinity, people began to picture the risen Christ as far away in heaven. In heaven, of course, he reigns as the Lord of the universe and the supreme judge of human behavior. And so, the risen Christ became not only "geographically" distant but psychologically less approachable. The imposing, even threatening, pictures of the Christ of glory on the ceiling of Romanesque chapels in medieval Catalonia make it unmistakably clear that the fear of the Lord Jesus is truly the beginning of wisdom. With believers still left on earth, and heaven quite far away, and all three divine persons "up there," there was a a a gap to be filled if people were to remain in contact with the divine. Enter the angels, especially that great adversary of Satan, Michael the Archangel. The prominence of Michael in Christian art and piety over the centuries is truly amazing. So, once again the gap had been bridged, there was a ladder of beings stretching from heaven to the needy mortals here on earth, a steady commerce of angels carrying God's help to us and carrying our prayers to the throne of God. This is where many people still are today in their thinking about angels.

The Teaching of St. Bernard

When I look at medieval Christianity's acceptance of angels, I have a special emotional problem to deal with. Probably the most influential person in the development of devotion to the guardian angels was none other than my patron saint, Bernard of Clairvaux. I find it hard to admit that he was in any way wrong. A few things things, however, help me.

First of all, with his great interest in Christian spirituality, Bernard, like others of his time, was immensely influenced by a writer considered in the Middle Ages to be a master of spirituality, none other than Pseudo-Dionysius the Areopagite, about whom we will talk in a minute. It was Pseudo-Dionysius whose *Celestial Hierarchy* was accepted for centuries as the classic work about angels. Secondly, Bernard was one of the medieval theologians who developed in detail the theory of mediation, the idea that God works to save humans through the various levels that make up "the great chain of being." Most importantly for Bernard was the mediation of Mary, the mother of Jesus.

No Christian theologian has written more eloquently about the role of Mary in bridging the gap between unworthy humans and her divine son. So, to have guardian angels as key mediators fitted very logically into Bernard's overall picture of mediation. Thirdly, and I think that this is not only consoling, but of considerable historical importance, Bernard's emphasis on mediators between God and humans did not diminish the sense Bernard had of Christ's love for women and men, and of Christ's continuing personal care for them. It was precisely this warmth of devotion to Christ that made Bernard the favorite medieval theologian of both Luther and Calvin. Guardian angels for Bernard, then, were not a substitute for Christ's loving presence, but a manifestation of it.

However, it was not only prayer and theology that fostered a sense of the reality and need of angels, so did philosophy and what for centuries was considered "science." Both ways of thinking presumed that there was a "great chain of being" that stretched from the greatest to the least of existent things. Since it was a chain – or sometimes the alternative image of a "ladder" was appealed to – it was necessary that no link, no step, be missing. An all-powerful and all-perfect creator would not have made an imperfect universe; so, the created world must be one in which the perfection of the creator is manifested in the perfection, i.e. the completeness of creation. All the gaps must be filled. Ordinary observation made it clear that this was true of life on this planet, from simplest forms to the human. But what links in the chain existed above humans, between them and God?

There was ample evidence that a considerable gap existed between humans and God; with our bodiliness and mortality, to say nothing of our sinfulness, we were far from divine. The great chain of being broke with us, unless there were other beings, neither bodily nor mortal like ourselves, beings confirmed in virtue, beings of intellect and will and freedom that far surpassed our own, in a word, unless there were angels. So, because they were obviously needed to make God's creation the complete piece of art it had to be, angels were accepted as a real, though usually not observable, part of creation.

Actually, in the early centuries of Christianity there were

numerous systems of thought that can be loosely gathered under
the umbrella term "Gnosticism." These dealt with "the gap" in
somewhat similar fashion, though they were not dealing with
what Christians meant by angels. For these esoteric ways of
explaining the universe, there were any number of forces or powers, good and bad ones, that filled the universe and carried power
from above to human life below. Gnostic wisdom consisted in
knowing how to manipulate these cosmic powers, usually
through some form of magic. This Gnosticism was a formidable
enemy of Christianity in its earliest days, an enemy against which
early apologists and theologians like St. Irenaeus directed their
writings.

What Augustine Taught

For Augustine of Hippo, probably the most influential theologian of western Christianity, angels formed an essential portion
of his vision of creation. God was distinguished from creation by
a number of factors, and by nothing more basic than the divine
immutability (the inability to change). Complete immutability
belonged only to God, and could only belong to God because it
was equated with total perfection. How could there be any
change in God, if the divine being already embraced infinity?

Creatures, on the contrary, were distinguished precisely by
their mutability; they were mutable in the two realms of space and
time. Material beings, humans included, were incessantly involved
in coming into being and going out of existence; their very bodiliness tied them to a world of spatial beings caught up in a net-
work of change. To be mutable also meant for humans to be "in
time," to never fully "be," but only be becoming, to exist only as
future becomes past, with only memory and imagination to provide an illusion of stability.

However, between God who is immutable and the bodily
world of mutability in both space and time, there was for
Augustine, as a logical part of a complete creation, a world of
beings who because they were not bodily were not spatially mutable, but though pure spirits were still mutable in time (or its equiv-

alent). These, of course, were the angels. As Augustine's thought passed on to shape the Christian belief and theology of the Middle Ages and beyond, so, too, did his explanation of the angels.

Another theologian who lived about the same time as Augustine also had immense influence on centuries of Christian thinking about angels. He is the one we have already referred to as "Pseudo-Dionysius." We do not know his real name, but he signed to his writings the name "Dionysius the Areopagite." Actually, the real Dionysius was the disciple of St. Paul and had lived more than five hundred years earlier; so today we refer to this sixth-century theologian as "Pseudo-Dionysius." However, the belief for centuries that the writings in question came from St. Paul's close disciple gave those writings an authority second only to the New Testament itself.

One of the writings of Pseudo-Dionysius was the *Celestial Hierarchy* in which he described in detail the nine choirs of angels, from seraphim down to "ordinary" guardian angels. This soon became the classic work on angels, and along with other writings by its author who unquestionably was a talented theologian, exerted unbelievable influence throughout the Middle Ages and into modern times.

More than any other piece of "evidence," the *Celestial Hierarchy* of Pseudo-Dionysius has shaped the way in which Christians have thought about the higher ranks of angels who surround the throne of God and the lower ranks of "ordinary" angels who at times are missioned to earth to watch over individual women and men, or even to watch over entire nations.

How, then, in the face of centuries of belief in and reflection about angels, religious and philosophical, could one have any doubt about their existence? One *could*, if the fundamental premise of these views is not true, the premise of a "great chain of being" that stretches from God down to the least of creatures and then back to God and within which is a gap between heaven and earth that needs to be bridged. If one does not see such a gap, and rightly or wrongly I do not, there would be no need for angels.

Yet it is hard to see how one can argue to their existence on the basis of their being needed, either to help us humans reach our destiny or to make "the great chain of being" complete. Perhaps it would be consoling to know that we have them as fellow travelers; but it may be even more consoling to recognize the guides and companions we do have on our journey, the risen Christ, the God he calls "Abba," and their Spirit. With them, what more could anyone want? And there is a whole other group of "non-earthly" companions about whom we'll talk later.

If God has been and still is in communication with us humans, wouldn't a logical way of going about it be to send angels as messengers, as representatives?

Chapter Two

UNDERSTANDING GOD'S PRESENCE

W ith all the changes going on in the world and even in the church, many of us have a hard time not being nostalgic about "the good old days" when life was simpler and clearer, when questions weren't being raised about things like guardian angels. Having a guardian angel by my side was, as I recall, a comforting experience. It was good to have a heavenly bodyguard, even if he was invisible and no apparent threat to any visible danger. More than that, there was, I suppose, a bit of self-esteem that came from being considered important enough by the Almighty to have one of the heavenly host assigned to me alone. Now, even though that sense of angel presence has long ago evaporated for me, I can understand why so many are attracted and comforted by the idea of watching and protecting angels.

Given the daily news stories and evening TV broadcasts, there is no need to elaborate on the dangers and problems that seem to be the pattern of life today. Still, as I have traveled around the country talking with people, most of whom would be considered "successful," I have been somewhat surprised and bothered by the level of anxiety they feel. For one thing, people consistently list "violence" as the number one problem facing us in the U.S. Broader than that is a prevalent feeling that "things just aren't going well" in our world. Values are disappearing, participation in the mainline Christian churches is declining, religious professionals no longer enjoy the unquestioned prestige that was theirs, the standard of living for the future seems threatened, etc., etc. Business and public life have become more hectic. Few would deny that "it's a jungle out there."

Politicians, of course, are all drawing attention to these negativities in our life, especially to the violence. Obviously, they do this for their own benefit, and they claim that if elected they will better the situation; but some of their "proposed remedies," such as pushing laws to allow the carrying of concealed handguns, do not give much promise of a better world. Elections are being won, and have been won during the past few decades, precisely by raising the level of people's fears, and along with that, the level of hostility for those who are subtly depicted as being "the problem."

An Army of God's Angels

In the midst of all this, it would be most comforting to know that despite all these threats to our happiness and our very lives, there was an army of God's angels fighting at our side against the forces of evil. Wasn't this what the prayer to Michael the archangel after Mass was all about: "Michael the Archangel, defend us in battle..."? And if we needed him then, there certainly is not less need today. So, belief in a guardian angel would clearly be an asset in today's world; even more an asset if that belief were true. Perhaps a guardian angel would not, probably could not, remove the threats to our well-being; but such a heavenly assistant might help us pick our way through the minefield, and at the least avoid being one of the casualties in the battle.

I can remember how believing in a guardian angel did give

me a sense of protection, part of a sense that "everything would work out" because of God's help. We certainly had problems when I was growing up; there was the Great Depression, when the desperate economic situation of millions was so apparent and when for years there did not seem to be any solution to the crisis. There was the rise of organized crime with its challenge to the dictum that crime does not pay. Then came Pearl Harbor, which shattered forever our illusion of being safe behind the barrier of two oceans. Yet, as I recall it, there was always the feeling that somehow we would muddle through, that we would make it, and I suspect that for many of us belief in a guardian angel was, without our realizing it, part of that basic optimism. However, I also remember how a human, FDR, played such an important role in reviving the spirits of the nation, not least by the famous speech, "We have nothing to fear except fear itself."

Without being politically partisan about it, I wonder if FDR was not in his own way "an angel," not necessarily in his own very human self, but in the role he played in our history, We'll talk more about this in another chapter; but it may be that the real "angels" in our lives are other humans. Earlier I mentioned that one of the greatest minds of Christian history, Dante, took the existence of angels for granted and gives a beautiful picture of the heavenly hosts surrounding the throne of God. But in his *Divine Comedy* it was not an angel that guided Dante himself on the journey to heaven; it was his beloved Beatrice. His love for her was the great saving grace of Dante's troubled life.

Does all this mean that devotion to my guardian angel was not really accomplishing something very important in my life, providing a basis for belief that life was good and would get better? Looking back on those years, I think that the guardian angel symbolized something extremely important: the protecting presence of God. I hadn't at that point recovered the sense of God's own immediate and constant presence to me. I had even confined Christ's presence to Mass and the reserved Eucharist. The one who was always at my side was none other than my guardian angel who was there as God's legate. But how, when I had something that important as a blessing in my life, have I come to my present suspicion that guardian angels are dispensable, indeed redundant?

Blessed Beyond Measure

To answer that, let me start way back in the days when "Angel of God, my guardian dear..." still meant a great deal to me. As I grew through childhood into youth, I was blessed beyond most mortals. My parents were of deep Christian faith, though each quite different in their faith. I had a mother for whom religion was not only the most important part of her life, it was the atmosphere in which her whole life was lived. Though it never substituted for her relationship with Christ and his Father, my mother's devotion to Mary, Christ's mother, was quite simply remarkable. Clearly, it mattered a great deal to her that she could pray to Mary, woman to woman. She probably figured Mary could understand what it meant to be the mother of us five boys. It was she who did so much to instill in me a devotion to Mary; and it was she who taught me "Angel of God, my guardian dear...."

My father was less given to multiple prayers, though he was a daily communicant. His Catholic faith meant for him a lasting commitment to social justice, a taken-for-granted commitment to providing dental care for hundreds of poor who in those days of the Great Depression had no hope of ever paying him. And it meant active involvement in our parish, acting informally as treasurer for the parish and as personal confidant and support for the pastor. For both parents, mature and intelligent faith was important; serious books and magazines were everywhere in the house, and on Sundays after Mass we were expected to discuss the sermon we had heard.

My education, taught for twelve years by devoted women religious in a little parish school, was one whose excellence still amazes me. Even religion classes were rather well taught, though the old Irish pastor who presided over my first five grades felt he needed to supplement school religion with catechism classes on Sunday. The pastor for my final seven years at home was a gentle man, intelligent and well educated, probably destined to be a bishop until his health broke. His sermons were always well prepared, and they often dealt with matters of doctrine, which was rather rare in those days when most preaching was moral exhortation and true homilies were non-existent. I learned to pray somewhat, was a faithful altar boy, and found my Catholic faith a gift to be treasured. I mention all this to emphasize that I was truly blessed in my religious background, and yet, as I was soon to discover, I was only vaguely aware of what is really at the heart of Christianity, indeed at the heart of all religious faith.

Fresh from high school, I left home to endure the rigors of a Jesuit novitiate, at least I was warned that there would be rigors. Apart from all the other contributions that that two-year experience made to my faith, one thing happened almost immediately, something that would forever alter my attitude on things angelic. What happened was that I was given as my first book for "spiritual reading," a slim volume by a French Jesuit, Raoul Plus, entitled *God With Us*. It dealt with something that I had never heard about before: God's *presence* to me. For weeks I read and reread that book, until the Novice Master finally insisted that I move on to some other reading.

As I described above, my Catholic upbringing was unusually good, the opportunity to understand my faith accurately was well beyond what most young persons could have enjoyed at that time. Yet, the presence of God was something completely new. Of course, I took for granted that God was creator, that God had to be wherever anything was, that divine power surrounded me and supported my very existence. But that was different from *presence*. Presence meant that God was interested in me. More than that, it meant that God was personally with me in friendship and that from that friendship I drew my deepest identity as a person. It meant that I was surrounded by, enveloped by, this love of me as a distinct individual person. It wasn't even that God lived in me; I lived in God.

I don't want to give the impression that God's presence to us humans is something quite obvious and easy to grasp. Just the opposite is true. That the transcendent reality we call "God" is personally involved with humans, concerned about those humans, is a profound mystery. From years of giving talks and teaching students about God, grace, and related topics, I know that an understanding of divine presence is difficult. I know it, too, from my own experience. Luckily we get glimmers of this divine-to-human relationship because of our own human experiences of love and friendship, of care and concern for one another. This experience of presence to one another is truly a sacrament of a loving God.

Reflection on what "presence" is all about in our dealings with one another does not dispel the mystery of God-for-us, but it can point us toward some understanding. Just as in our human relationships, presence is other than mere spatial location; divine presence means something other than that God's creative power is everywhere, sustaining creation in its existence. When I am present to you, somehow I am in your awareness; my presence to you is not where I am located spatially; it occurs in your consciousness. Moreover, my presence to you, which is more or less a giving of myself to you, depends on my willingness and ability to let you know what I am all about and your willingness to listen and accept my self-giving. The level of presence is conditioned at both ends by our free choice to communicate or not.

God Communicates With Us

God's presence to us functions in much the same way. In the mystery we call "divine revelation," God has for millennia been communicating with humans, and dependent upon the receptiveness to that communication which is faith. God has been *for* people. Until rather recently, we Christians limited such self-giving revelation by God to the period of Old Testament Israel and to Christianity. While we still regard the religious experience available to Christians as in some fashion unique, we have in recent decades come to the realization that such experience is something shared by humans in many other of the world's great religions. Christians do not have a monopoly on God.

Suppose we accept, in faith of course, that God has been and still is in communication with us humans, which makes God personally present to us. Wouldn't a very logical way of going about it be to send angels as messengers, as representatives? After all, even in human affairs, "really important" people who are busy about many things and manage the large-scale activities of our human life, use representatives to keep in touch with the mass of us. God's use of angelic mediators would, then, make great good sense, since God has to be concerned about the entire universe and can't immediately take care of each human's affairs. But is the God revealed by Jesus a top-level administrator who efficiently delegates tasks? Or is God, as Jesus describes his heavenly Father, immediately involved even with the flowers and the birds, so that not a single sparrow falls to earth without his Father's knowledge?

Of course, if the universe (and, in parallel fashion, the church) is structured like a ladder, with power and life flowing down from God through a succession of mediators, the gap between heaven and earth would have to be filled with angelic mediators. The proof for angels seems to hinge on the existence or non-existence of this gap. But again, to be honest, I must admit that it is altogether possible that there are angels, and that God uses them to assist us toward our destiny. If there are angelic guardians protecting and guiding us, they would truly be a "word" about the God who lovingly cares for us; they would be a means of God communicating with us and so making God constantly present to us, just as our human words to one another are what allow us to be present to one another.

A Sense of the Divine Presence

I think that exactly something like this was happening to me in the years when a guardian angel at my side was part of my awareness of life. This angelic companion did not come and go the way that even the risen Christ did, being with us in Eucharist and then being "away" for the rest of the time. It was precisely in this constant being-with-me that the guardian angel symbolized the unbroken attention of God to me. While I never explicitly reflected on it, for I had not yet thought that much about God's presence, my guardian angel was the implicit message of God's presence.

Perhaps, because God's presence is so mysterious and unbelievable, it was necessary that a devotion to the guardian angel be the first step in creating a sense of divine presence in our lives. Without this "preliminary" experience of God being with and for us, we might not have been able later to glimpse the wonder of God being immediately involved in our lives. So, even if there never was an angel at my side, devotion to my guardian angel was something real and very important in my Christian faith.

I suspect that this was the case because of an incident that occurred many years ago now. Along with about thirty others, I was in Spain at a meeting about theology and prayer. In the course of our discussion, the question of angels and devils arose. As you might expect, there was considerable disagreement, with some skeptical about the existence of angels and others arguing for their reality. Finally, the group appealed to one of the participants who, because he was one of the leading New Testament scholars in the world, commanded everyone's respect. In his opinion, did guardian angels really exist? I'll never forget his answer: "I don't see anything in the bible that indicates clearly the existence of guardian angels; but I pray to mine every day."

Given how mysterious and wondrous is God's presence to us humans and how difficult to understand and appreciate, it is altogether possible that, for all of us, the devotion to a guardian angel has been a necessary preparation. It is so easy to confuse God's presence with God's "being there," to put God into our space and time. But if God isn't "being there," what does God's presence mean? It means simply that God is aware of us, communicating to us in various ways, being for us in love and concern, offering a friendship that alone can ultimately lead us to our personal fulfillment, taking the initiative and calling us into this unbelievable relationship. We certainly can call this "grace" because it is so absolutely gratuitous, and we have come to realize that this is the most important dimension of grace, "uncreated grace."

At the point of my initially becoming aware of God's presence to me, I had not even begun to link all this with the Holy Spirit. I did know that God's Spirit was somehow involved with God's being with me, but it would be long years afterward before I even began to sort out my faith understanding of God's Spirit. I am still only at the beginning. Even more surprising to me now as I look back was that Christ's risen presence to us was not yet part of that first breakthrough insight. I remember that when he gave the book to me, the Novice Master warned me that the kind of presence of which the book spoke pertained only to *divine* presence. Obviously that would apply also to Christ in so far as he was God, but not in so far as he was the risen human Jesus.

What his remarks seemed to imply was that I could justifiably have a sense of the presence of my guardian angel, because he was always "here"; but I could not have this same awareness of Christ, for as human he was in heaven. As I look back now, I realize that he was capsuling the very process of what had happened in the early centuries of the church. In Christians' imagination Jesus the Christ, risen and glorified, was gradually seen to reside in heaven rather than to be constantly present to believers here on earth. Certainly his presence in the eucharistic action and in the reserved Blessed Sacrament was very real, but it was a presence (by which they were really understanding "spatial location") that was limited to Eucharist and did not extend to the rest of one's daily life. And just as angels like Michael filled in for the "absent" Christ, so devotion to my guardian angel supplied for Christ not being with me apart from the precious moments of Eucharist.

Rediscovering the Presence of Christ

However, one must be very careful in trying to recapture the faith experience of Christians in the past, particularly their experience of relationship to Christ. While it is true that they thought of the risen Christ as being in heaven, they also maintained a sense that he was aware of and in contact with them, even beyond his being with them in Eucharist. There was a certain inconsistency in that, an inconsistency that became apparent in the attempts to explain Christ's eucharistic presence. But one of the clearest reflections of the imaginative distancing of Christ from earth was centuries of artistic representation of the risen Christ. For almost a thousand years, until the painting of Giotto in the thirteenth century, Jesus was not depicted against an earthly background. Yet, from about the thirteenth century until now, there has been a gradual regaining of the early Christian awareness that Jesus' "resurrection" means his being with us in history rather than his "going away." And from the middle of this century, there has come a fuller appreciation of Christ's constant presence to believers, an awareness that drew from the experience of eucharistic presence and, I am suggesting, from the belief in a guardian angel. The whole church is still in the process of rediscovering the abiding presence of the risen Christ, which may be the most important cause of the change taking place today in the life of the church.

Like many other Catholics I had inherited an unquestioning belief in the presence of Christ during the celebration of the Eucharist and a continuing presence in the reserved Blessed Sacrament. That belief was the underpinning of some level of religious experience of Christ's presence, but it was confined to Eucharist, to Mass or to "visits to the Blessed Sacrament." Once one left the church building, one was no longer in Christ's presence. A guardian angel still helped bridge the gap between myself and Christ "up in heaven" for most of the day. It was only in the years when I first began formal study of theology, that European theologians and biblical scholars published the books that altered our whole perspective on the resurrection of Christ and allowed us to realize that the risen Christ is constantly present, in the full sense of that term, to all who accept that presence in faith.

Christ's "real presence" does pertain to Eucharist, but more basically it has to do with Christ's constant presence to those of faith. This in no way detracts from the reality or importance of Christ being present to the believing community as it celebrates Eucharist, any more than a married couple's abiding sense of loving and being loved takes away from their presence to one another as they make love. As this sense of Christ being with us has grown, it is slowly dawning on us that there is no gap between heaven and earth that needs to be bridged.

Though it took me quite some time to work out the relationship of what at first seemed to be two presences, the presence of God and the presence of Christ, being Christian came to mean living with awareness of Christ's presence to me as "the sacrament of the presence of God." I did not yet realize it—things were changing much too fast—that what was happening in my faith understanding was part of a massive shift which was starting to take place in Christian faith and life.

Clearly, my new awareness came only because many others had already come to this realization, because for several decades a whole series of awakenings had been quietly taking place among Christian scholars. Really, it would be more correct to speak of "re-awakening," for it was precisely by careful study of Christianity's origins and historical evolution, by reflecting on the most central elements of Christian tradition, that insight into the reality of Christianity was gained.

Remembering again that in resurrection Jesus did not leave our world but became the risen Christ present to believers "to the end of the world," allowed us to recover a sense of the church being "body of Christ"; it allowed us to experience Eucharist as encounter with the divine and to integrate Eucharist with the rest of life, and it paved the way for Vatican II describing the church as a community, a family, that dwells in the presence of God.

What Happened to Guardian Angels?

And what happened to my guardian angel? Quite simply he was displaced. I never thought about it, but everything that a guardian angel was intended to do was now done by Christ himself—and then some. Constant and totally faithful companionship, understanding patience with my humanity (one thing angels cannot do is appreciate being human!) infinite power (his Spirit) to help me to my destiny.

It wasn't so much that the guardian angel—and angels in general—disappeared. What has disappeared is the gap between heaven and earth, which was the reason why we thought there should be angels. We don't need a bridge to God, God is with us. Very truly, "heaven" is here. We are not yet fully into that new life we refer to with the word "heaven"; we will have to pass through death to be completely part of it, but death will not be a matter of going someplace else. If "heaven" is being with God, we already are with God, unless we refuse to accept the friendship offered us through Christ. Moreover, God works with us, present to us throughout our lives, to insure that we reach this final goal. As the popular hymn has it: "If God is for us, who can be against...."

Let me briefly mention now (and then develop it at length later) something else that is connected with our moving away from the notion of a gap between heaven and earth. For centuries, indeed for millennia, most of our cultures have been working with an up-and-down image of reality. Power, intelligence, beauty, goodness—all were imagined to be in "up there" in a full and perfect form. They gain a gradually diminishing expression as they are filtered on down to the ordinary created world and ordinary people.

So also in our way of imagining human society, we still speak of those in power as people who are "on top." This ascending/ descending ladder has been enshrined in patterns of culture that we called "patriarchy" or "hierarchy," and that were described in great detail by writers like Pseudo-Dionysius. The link with the imagery of a "great chain of being" is obvious. Such underlying symbols of reality have immense influence; they not only structure our human consciousness, they motivate our decisions and shape our actions. We think and act the way we do because we think that's what "reality" is.

Today an incredibly revolutionary shift is occurring in cultures across the world. The up-and-down vertical image of reality is giving way to a horizontal image that is connected with ideas like "community," "equality," "consensus," "cooperation," and "sharing," rather than with "ruler," "boss," "superior/inferior," or "giving orders." The shift is happening painfully because the vested interests of those "on top" are being threatened; very few people who possess power give it up willingly. The very vocal and often harsh expressions of this "law and order" mentality make it clear that there is a strong gut reaction to what is happening.

A Discipleship of Equals

This massive cultural shift has already begun to have its effect on our religious understandings. Just one indication is the prominence in the proceedings of the Second Vatican Council of the word "communio" (the Latin word for "sharing"), and the disputes going on in official circles ever since regarding the importance of this notion in interpreting the intent and application of the Council. If the horizontal imagery of family, of a discipleship of equals, of genuine community, all grounded in awareness that God is present with us rather than being above us in heaven, were to become accepted, then things like domination, hierarchy, submission, and control would be seen as incompatible with Christianity. In such a view of reality, where there is not "up and down," and where consequently there is no gap between what is up and what is down, one wonders where gap-filling angels fit into the picture.

But if all this is true, why are angels so popular today? I wonder if it is not because people for the most part have not discovered the reality of divine presence, or that it is simply too good to be true. I do think that there is an evident hunger for this presence. Many people seem to be searching for it, looking for the breakthrough of higher power into our world. Isn't this to some extent the tantalizing appeal of *The Celestine Prophecy?*

We sometimes hear people who are spiritually inclined say things like "God is within me" or "there is a spark of divinity in all of us." They are certainly getting at something true, but the mystery of God's presence to us in Christ goes far beyond God being wherever we are. I fear that the gospel of divine presence has yet to be preached to most people, but I also believe that this is a blessed moment in history when we are aware that this is the gospel we must preach. Maybe, just maybe, people's attraction to a reality that is spiritual, to majesty beyond all our earthly wealth and power, in a word, to angels, will prepare people to hear that gospel, to embrace and treasure the God who is for them, and to enjoy a hope and peace they never before had, even if they believed they had a guardian angel.

Several perceptive social analysts have observed that ours is a world threatened by a loss of the very notion of "spirit." We are swamped by the propaganda of a massive goods-producing, goods-marketing enterprise that for lack of a better name we refer to as "capitalism." Without entering into the disputes about the benefits or evils of capitalism as an economic system, it seems quite clear that with this whole arrangement of human work and life, has come the pervasive judgment that humans will be happy in proportion to their material possessions. Perhaps many people sense the threat in all this to the very notion that humans are meant to be persons, i.e., incarnated *spirits,* and that being spirit is ultimately more important than having things. Maybe the interest in angels is part of our interest in remaining human.

I wonder if the present interest
in angels would endure if people
began to realize how God's Spirit
is truly creative and ever present.

Chapter Three

WE SHARE GOD'S
"SPIRIT POWER"

In only one week recently, three things happened that made me aware of just how prevalent interest in angels is. 1) At my daughter's urging I visited a psychic fair and saw there a rather large display of books about angels; 2) our local newspaper, not particularly noteworthy for in-depth coverage of religious matters, had a lengthy feature article on the role of angels in people's lives; and 3) at the checkout line at the nearby supermarket I noticed that the cover article of *The National Enquirer* dealt with angels.

The first of these events in particular somewhat puzzled, even startled me, and perhaps led me a bit closer to understanding the present fascination with these winged spirits. If you've ever visited a psychic shop, you've noticed the esoteric collection of materials that attach to the notion of "new age." So, I was prepared at this particular psychic fair to see every variety of crystal and amulet, to be surrounded by book racks filled with Castaneda and *The Celestine Prophecy* and *The Egyptian Wisdom of Seth,* to be well-nigh overcome with smoking incense, and to discover that the feature of the day was a famous traveling palm reader. But what was a large collection of books about angels doing in the midst of all this? I had always associated angels with my early Catholic upbringing, something that reminded me of a religious past that had given way to the revisionist thinking and practice of the past half century; but here were the angels prominently embraced as part of the New Age.

Then the connection began to dawn on me. All the things in this psychic fair, most of which were part of the regular items of sale in the rather large store where the fair was held, had to do with "spirit power." Crystals and fragrances and Castaneda and even palm reading dealt with, or at least were thought to deal with, hidden energies, "vibes," supra-bodily though embodied forces. Here at the heart of the most evident and fringe display of the New Age was a distillation of centuries, nay millennia, of human belief in unseen but powerful forces that worked for good or ill in human experience.

Harnessing God's Spirit

People were searching for what humans had always been seeking: a key to controlling the powers that influenced their lives, hoping to find the secret of harnessing the "good spirits," and hoping to discover how to avoid the influence of "evil spirits." Even though centuries of Old Testament exhortation tried to wean the Israelites from belief in such magical solutions to life, even though the gospel accounts of Jesus' temptations in the desert tell how he repudiated magic in his refusal to change stones to bread, even though philosophers like Giordano Bruno and countless scores of accused "witches" were put to death for their supposed involvement in the world of the supra-human, the underground belief in and practice of esoteric contact with the realms of the spirit has remained strong up to the present day. Not even psychoanalysis with its "scientific" explanation for the psychic dimension of us humans has been able to dispel the suspicion of people that we live in the midst of very real psychic power that we only vaguely understand.

Paradoxically, I agree with this suspicion. As a matter of fact, for me it is not a suspicion but a conviction that power far beyond the human surrounds us and is at our disposal. But it is not the power reflected in a psychic fair. The power that is meaningful for me and that makes all the other claims to spirit-power weak and irrelevant is what Christian faith calls "The Holy Spirit." That is said, not to pass any judgment on those who place faith in those other sources of power, not a complacent claim to superior understanding, but to wonder what would happen if so many who are eagerly searching for spirit power could believe that Christ's Spirit works with us to transform life and overcome the evils that threaten our future.

Is it, I wonder, a mere coincidence that at this moment in history, when millions are turning away from traditional religious groups and to "new age" movements, that we have witnessed in the Christian churches the phenomenon of Charismatic Renewal? Yes, there are some forms of this charismatic development that may be questionable, that are narrowly gnostic and arrogantly exclusive of all but "the inner circle," or that are linked with ultra-conservative political agendas; but the broader charismatic movement is something quite other. It has manifested itself across the globe in an awakened interest in prayer, in care and concern for the disadvantaged, in an embracing of discipleship and responsibility for the earth and its people. It seems that God's Spirit is being manifested in our day far beyond what has been the case for a long time. But in what ways does one, with some assurance that one is not imagining things or projecting one's own hopes and expectations, experience the presence of God's Spirit? The question is as old as Christianity.

How We Experience the Spirit

Though it took some time to think through, it was not all that difficult to add to the awareness of God's presence an awareness of the presence of the human risen Christ. After all, the experience of Mass had already given Catholics (and in a slightly different way those Protestants who celebrated liturgies of The Lord's Supper or

Holy Communion) a sense of Christ's eucharistic presence. As we saw, this could now be extended to Christ's presence to people.

Knowing exactly what to do about the Holy Spirit was another matter. It is hard to find an element in Christian belief that has been less developed theologically and consequently less clarified for people through teaching and preaching. We do have the language of creeds that speak of three divine persons, Father, Son, and Holy Spirit. From the beginning, Christians have been baptized with these names. But how the word "person" applies to God's Spirit is probably misunderstood by most Christians or vaguely understood at best. My guess is that most people never give it any thought at all.

However, as we mentioned, there is a worldwide resurgence of attention to God's Spirit and with it a new focus on pneumatology, the careful study of this Spirit. Where exactly it will lead is not yet clear, but it is already evident that it cannot be separated from our theology about Christ or about the church. God's Spirit is Christ's Spirit, the animating source of his risen existence; and this same Spirit is also the indwelling animating principle of the life of the Christian church. A few things about God's Spirit are clear from scripture and from two thousand years of Christian faith: God's Spirit is God's infinite and creative power; God's Spirit is life-giving in the deepest sense because this Spirit is God's self-giving love. But what can this mean to us humans who still live with such a different notion of "power"? Is it anything more than words, to say that the ultimate power in creation is love?

This was another place where belief in the angels was much easier to handle. We did have a largely unformulated belief that God's Spirit had something to do with God's power to help and save us. We spoke about receiving the Holy Spirit in baptism and confirmation. Still it was in the ongoing process of daily life, trying to make good moral choices in the midst of temptations, working to put faith into practice, that we needed more "tangible" help. Angels were exactly the kind of beings God would logically employ to do this. Next to God they were the most powerful beings around, much more powerful than we poor frail humans.

Not only was our individual guardian angel a superior being, given to us to help withstand the powers of hell, but there were specially powerful archangels like Michael who could contend with the mightiest forces of evil. Hadn't Michael already done this in the great cosmic conflict in which he overthrew Lucifer and sent him forever into hell?

We have long since abandoned the practice, but when I was growing up and for many years thereafter, we recited this prayer to Michael after each Mass: "Be our protection against the wickedness and snares of the devil...Michael the archangel, defend us in battle." The battle, of course, was with all the powers of evil that we seemingly confronted each day, evil that threatened to deprive us of our eternal destiny. It was only years later that I learned why we began to recite this prayer after Mass. It went back to the days of Pope Pius IX when with the emergence of modern Italy under leaders like Garibaldi, the Papal States were conquered and forever taken away from the control of the Pope.

At that time such a loss of the territory over which the Pope had long ruled as king seemed a catastrophe, brought about by the evils of liberalism, democracy, and secularism that threatened the kingdom of God. And so Catholics prayed each day that Michael would protect them against all these modern evils. We have since come to realize that loss of the Papal States was most likely a great blessing, for it freed the papacy from involvements with international politics and wars that had kept it from being the religious force it is meant to be.

A Sign of God's Concern

So, the presence of angels like Michael was a clear sign of God's concern for us humans, for it meant that God's power worked through these higher spirits, and through them God's power was at our disposal. Obviously, this was a comforting thought for people, for most people are relatively powerless in our world, at least by ordinary standards. And I cannot but wonder if this is one reason for the popularity of angels today. Confronted with massive structures of power, economic, political, military, what is there that the ordinary people, even in a country like the United States, can do to control their lives? Still, given the fact that the great majority of people do not reflect much on the large-scale national or international structures that affect their lives, and so do not relate the power of those structures to the power of God or God's angels, it seems to me that another viewpoint explains why so many people link angels with the manifestation of God's power in our world.

Is God's Action Extraordinary?

Almost instinctively people expect God's influence on human life, if there is such influence, to take place through extraordinary happenings. Reports of miracles inevitably draw crowds to the place of the supposed miracles. Just let rumors start that a statue in some church is weeping (presumably for our human sinfulness), and a massive traffic jam is likely to ensue as people flock to see this newest intervention of God. That miracles, happenings that can find no ordinary human explanation, are possible is not the issue. There certainly are some things, probably many things, that defy our human understanding. But the simple fact is that people do not expect God to work through what is ordinary. That God would "intervene" to overcome evil through ordinary human beings like ourselves seems altogether too commonplace, therefore ineffective, but that God should act through angels, now there is something more appropriate!

So, rather than settling for a secularism that excludes God from human history and presumes that we humans can adequately handle our problems, we have once more turned to belief in angels. That makes good sense, since it has become unavoidably patent that we cannot handle our affairs—two great world wars plus an unending series of regional conflicts have made that clear. Why, then, would I still maintain that angels are redundant? Quite simply because we have constantly at our disposal, constantly working more intimately in those lives than any angel could, the very power of God, God's own Spirit.

That we today are a bit vague in our thinking about the Spirit should come as no surprise. For the past two thousand years, though there has been constant mention of "the Holy Spirit" and people have been baptized in the name of this Spirit; though millions of Christians have signed themselves several times daily "in the name of the Father and of the Son and of the Holy Spirit," and though the doctrine of the Trinity is at the very heart of Christian belief, there has been little advance in our thinking about this Holy Spirit. Today there are clear signs that this may be changing, that there will finally emerge an adequate pneumatology, a theology of the Spirit; but this remains for the moment a hope rather than a realization.

At the same time, we have gained enough awareness of God's Spirit, which is also Christ's Spirit, to challenge some of our previous understandings of "grace" and of the function of angels. Simply put, what we now appreciate about the role of the Spirit in our lives does not leave much room for the function we assumed angels played. But what is it we know about God's Spirit that seems to replace the need for guardian angels?

During the (roughly) twelve centuries when the people of Israel were experiencing the intervention of God in their history, and their prophets and priests and historians and wise persons were producing the literature we call "the Old Testament" or "the Hebrew Bible," mention of the Spirit of God does not come to prominence until about 600 BCE. The great prophet Ezekiel is the first one really to develop an idea of God's Spirit, a spirit of creative power, a life-giving spirit, a spirit that works in the prophets and through them to lead reluctant Israel toward its God-given destiny. In Ezekiel's vision of the dry bones with its hope of Israel's restoration as a people, we get the bible's first hint of belief in "resurrection": The dispersed bones of dead Israel (the chosen people in Babylonian exile), that lie strewn on the valley floor, again form skeletons and then assume flesh and life as Israel is resurrected. All of this is done by the power of God's life-giving Spirit.

The Spirit is God's power manifested in creation; it is the power that accompanies the word of the prophet and makes that

word cause what it proclaims. While it always accompanies God's
Word, God's Spirit is not exactly the same kind of power. The
power of Word has more to do with "shaping" reality, giving
things form, specifying human knowledge by ideas, giving society structure by laws; the power of Spirit has more to do with the
force we associate with love, with the impulse that motivates people to action, with the urge of people to link up with others and
form community. Historically, Christian faith and theology have
associated God's Spirit with divine love. In its own way it is the
dynamism in creation. It is, to put it technically, the eschatologi-
cal Spirit. Moreover, God's Spirit is not only the dynamism in creation, more specifically it is the source of all life, organic life and
conscious life.

God's Spirit in Creation

Not that he is dealing with the Holy Spirit in his great book,
The Phenomenon of Man, but Teilhard de Chardin speaks of
something there that has helped me a great deal in reflecting on
the role of God's Spirit in creation. Teilhard introduces the notion
of "radial energy" which, if I can attempt an over-simplified explanation, is the driving force behind the gradual evolution of the
universe. Radial energy, as Teilhard spoke of it, is an uncontain-
able power, always moving what already is to something more,
pushing material creation to life and then to personal consciousness in humans and toward the ultimate realization of creation
that Teilhard called "the Omega Point." This creative dynamism is
never satisfied, short of the Omega Point, but incessantly leads
creation to its destiny. Basically it is person-power, even in the
millennia prior to humans' appearance in the evolutionary process
when it is thrusting material reality towards the breakthrough of
consciousness. Once humans appear on the scene, radial energy
drives history toward an ever-greater level of consciousness and
personal realization. This notion of radial energy seems to me to
provide some analogy to the pervasive creative power of God's
life-giving Spirit.

This insight into God's Spirit as life-giving takes on concrete definition in Jesus. The Spirit lies at the very origin of Jesus' human existing and human identity. Mary is told, "the Spirit of God will overshadow you and so the one to be born of you will be called the son of God." This Spirit moves Jesus to his prophetic mission, empowers him in that mission to testify to God, his Abba, by prophetic proclamation and wonder-working, and accompanies him in his transition through death to new life, new life that is precisely and completely life in the Spirit. Easter and Pentecost are one single event, for Jesus is risen in order to share this Spirit of new life.

Admittedly, it is a lot easier for us to think about angels; we can even picture them in human form. It does seem to me, though, that we have some analogies from our human experience that can help a little bit in grasping the reality of God's Spirit. We talk about certain people as having a lot of spirit; they are spirited. We even at times call some of them "inspired." We know that certain groups have a lot of spirit, while other groups are "dead." And we know that these spirited groups are often that way because of certain charismatic individuals who inspire the entire group. All too infrequently we have public figures, in society or in the church, who seem to breathe new life into our human existing, who inspire us to new dreams and new creativity.

We Share a Great Gift

In Christianity, we are meant to share not just the enthusiasms and ideals of such inspired leaders, we are meant to share God's own "inspiration," God's own Spirit. Jesus, of course, did possess this Spirit of his Abba in unique and full form; in his very existing he was Spirit-filled. So, his thinking and desires and decisions and actions always grew out of this Spirit that he knew he shared with his heavenly Father. That was why, too, he was aware that the things he did were not only his, but also God's; and why when his enemies accused him of working wonders through the power of the devil he accused them of blaspheming against God's Spirit.

In somewhat similar and derived fashion, we humans can

share this "mindedness" of God and the creative power that flows from such mindedness. We can be moved by God's (and Christ's) own Spirit and so live that way right into unending life after earthly death. We are meant to begin our life beyond even here, for we already share that unending life to the extent that we freely allow God's Spirit to move in us on this earth.

Because this is such an incredible access to power, why would we need angels to provide for us? Could this Spirit also work through the agency of mediating angels? Of course, but I must admit that that seems a bit redundant. And I cannot but wonder whether the present interest in angels would endure if people began to realize how God's Spirit is truly creative. It seems even more redundant when we realize that there are already millions of personal beings who mediate this Spirit. Those beings are us. God's Spirit touches each of us through others, just as we transmit that Spirit to others by sharing the gospel of Jesus as God's Christ.

Still, questions about the reality of angels have not left me. We have learned in recent decades to do our theological reflection out of the shared experience of believing women and men; and people's belief in angels cannot simply be dismissed. Let me give just one example; this past summer when I was teaching, as I regularly do, a course on Christology to a group of graduate students, we necessarily dealt in class with the mystery of God's Spirit. We had said nothing about angels. One morning midway through the course, as I was eating breakfast in the student cafeteria, three of these students joined me and—I don't remember exactly how—the conversation turned to angels. They were soon aware of my hesitations about angels, but without exception they claimed that their experience argued for the existence of their respective guardian angels.

One, for instance, said that repeatedly and with consistent success, she uses her guardian angel to carry messages to people at a distance. Another has no need for an alarm clock; her angel faithfully wakes her at the desired time. Mind you, these were mature people with an educated approach to their faith; they had been hearing in class about the role of Christ's Spirit in our lives; and yet belief in their guardian angels remained firm and active. Who am I to say that they are mistaken?

It is clear that a positive effort
should be made to move Catholics
from a devotional spirituality
to a spirituality bound up with
active eucharistic participation.

Chapter Four

WE ARE ALL SACRAMENTS OF GOD

Apart from a certain curiosity about the current interest in angels, why bother spending so much time talking about them, especially if they are, as I am suggesting, rather redundant? In the long run, would it make all that much difference whether people believed in guardian angels and trusted in their help or not? Couldn't we just take them or leave them? Wouldn't life and even one's relation to God go on just about the same? I don't think so. Actually I believe that something very basic and important is at stake, something that is at the very root of the shifts taking place today in our religious understandings and daily lives. And the current focus on angels could be a distraction, even a cop-out from the opportunities and responsibilities of this new developing situation. That is quite a claim, but I think that it's justified.

Toward the end of the eighteenth century, Immanuel Kant, a German philosopher whose influence on modern thought has been immense, drew attention to the way we humans think about space and time. His own explanation is quite complicated, but to oversimplify it, one could say that space and time as we think of them, and even more importantly as we imagine them, do not exist. Take "time," for example. We are so used to clocks and measuring time the way we do, that we take for granted that there are minutes and hours. Really, as a moment's reflection indicates, these are artificial divisions to which we have become accustomed. We could divide up the day's passage in other ways. Or why have a week of only seven days? There is nothing intrinsic about a seven-day week. Even more fundamental is the way we imagine time as a line, as if past and present and future exist one after the other, when really the only thing that exists is a moving moment, which when it no longer exists, we remember as the past, and when it has not yet existed, we imagine it as the future. Our memories and imaginations create the time-line and allow us to situate happenings one after another in our consciousness. We know that many cultures have not thought about time in this linear fashion; rather, they think of it is an eternally recurring circle, so that in the final analysis we are not timewise going anywhere except around and around.

Creatures of Space and Time

Space also is largely a creation of our imagining and thinking. We today think about space in a very different way than did the people of Jesus' day or the people for centuries before and after his time. In biblical times humans thought of the earth being covered by a hemisphere, the "firmament," which provided a barrier against the chaotic waters, that unless dammed, would flood and destroy the earth. In this firmament were embedded the various heavenly bodies that assumed different positions in the sky as this firmament revolved. This view of "the heavens" was gradually refined as earth was thought to be surrounded by a number of concentric spheres whose complex motions explained the various astronomical movements. However, the basic impression of living in enclosed space remained unchallenged until almost modern times. Today, we have a different awareness of space. For us the sky is unlimited and we are not protected by a heavenly shield. Moreover, artists and architects are aware of the subtle ways in which "space" can be created in our consciousness and how this can affect our experience and even our moods.

What does all this have to do with angels? Angels were thought to be part of this whole system of revolving spheres. Medieval theologians saw the moving of the heavenly bodies to be one of the functions of those angels assigned to take care of creation. Today we think about the stars and planets and their motion in a very different way; not even those who take angels for granted and are devoted to their guardian angel, think of angels moving the sun or the moon or the planets.

There is another "dimension" to space, however, where most of us continue to think of some forces like angels at work. Humans have always imagined—and still do—that behind or beneath the visible world we experience (and of which we are a part), there exists another layer of reality. That is the really real world; that is where hidden forces are causing the events in our world. What we see and hear and touch is a screen that hides this truer reality. In people's religious beliefs, it is in this "behind the scenes" world that God is at work, where graces are given to help us in times of decision, where both good angels and bad angels function to influence our lives.

Looking for Deeper Meaning

The bible, the liturgy, and to some extent our ordinary experience give us glimpses of this real world, but they do so as a code that needs to be deciphered. So it was that for centuries scholars used the allegorical method to discover what they considered to be the real meaning of things and events behind immediate experience. The literal, more obvious, meaning of a biblical passage or of a liturgical ritual was not its "deep" meaning. To discover the more ultimate word that God was speaking through these media, one had to reflect on the "spiritual meaning" that lay beneath the surface. Nature itself needed to be probed in this manner, so that underneath appearances one could see how God was really at work and discover what was really happening. As medieval thinkers expressed it, God has given us two books to learn to read as God's word, the book of the Bible and the book of Nature.

In this perspective, God's workings with humans, God's providence, was often linked with people's understandings of the magical forces at work in the universe. While people professed their belief that God did not work through magic, they nonetheless had many religious rituals to which they attached an almost magical efficacy: a certain prayer repeated a particular number of times (nine was a favorite), a pilgrimage to a particular sacred place, and wearing a blessed medal. Such were believed to have an almost automatic effect, to influence God to grant a certain request. Or if God did not work magically—and scripture insisted strongly that God did not—at least God was constantly involved behind the scenes bringing about the results in people's lives that was "the will of God." Still today, for example, when people lose their jobs or get sick, they wonder why God is punishing them; as if God working behind the scenes had something to do directly with their unemployment.

A Negative Influence

This mentality of situating God's influence on humans at some hidden level of reality, screened off by the visible world we experience, has been a negative influence on the way Christians have thought about and participated in eucharistic worship. For centuries, most people's attention at Mass has focused on the moment of consecration, the moment when "the words of institution" (This is my body; this is my blood) were pronounced over the bread and wine.

Admittedly, people did not claim to understand how this changed ordinary bread and wine into the body and blood of the risen Christ, but it was taken for granted that it must be something "beneath the appearances," for, despite the appearances, one accepted in faith that the reality was no longer bread and wine. What was *really* going on was God's hidden action; and the presence of the risen Christ, the true meaning of what was happening, the saving effect of the Eucharist, had to do with this hidden level of divine activity.

Today, these views of divine providence, of the way that God works in our world, are changing. The change, while rather slow, is a change of immense proportions, a change that lies at the very bottom of religious beliefs and practices. In answer to the question: "What is God doing, if anything, to influence human life?" (in religious language "to save us"), we are starting to realize that the key is God's presence to our lives in and through the presence of the risen Christ. This answer is saying much more, however, than what God is doing. It is saying that the created world, and humans in particular, are "for real." But isn't that what we always thought, that we humans are real and living in a real world?

Yes and no. We are pretty well convinced that we actually exist, but is the life and the self we experience as "really real" as the behind-the-scenes world? We are moving away from responding "no" to that question and realizing that what is right in front of us, what we see and hear and touch is the only created reality there is. We do try to probe more deeply into the forces—physical or psychological or social—that are at work in this immediately perceived reality, and that explain why what is happening is happening. However, this is a probing into *this* reality and not the discovery of another reality. There is no behind-the-scenes world; "what you see is what you get."

God's Presence Is Reality

Religiously, this leads us to the notion of "sacramentality." What sacramentality is all about is that God's presence, which gives ultimate meaning to our experiences and ourselves, occurs in our ordinary daily experience. Obviously, there can be more apparent situations of divine presence in some extraordinary things that happen, in moments of danger or discovery or success; but God's presence is not something that comes and goes except in so far as we are more or less conscious of it. We talked earlier about this presence; what needs to be underlined here is that this is not something "behind the scenes." God's self-gift to us in presence is a great mystery, but that does not mean that it is hidden.

Indeed, presence demands that it be known, be revealed to us, that it be grounded in communication between God and ourselves. This communication takes place in what is right in front of us, in our experiences, and most especially in our experience of certain people who are truly "word of God" for us and in our experience of being "word of God" for others.

As we become aware of this sacramentality of our experience, of ourselves, of the happenings in our lives, of the people with whom we deal, the accompanying awareness of God being "for us" inexorably transforms that experience. What seemed ordinary and unimportant, unimportant precisely because it was ordinary, now can be seen as an ongoing relationship with God, which is, as Jesus described it in one of his parables, "the pearl of great price." There are no unimportant people, there is no "secular" world that is not touched and made sacred by God's presence, though there can be sinful elements in the world that result from purposeful rejection of this presence.

Again, a gap is disappearing. There is no need to bridge the distance between the observable everyday reality of our lives and some behind-the-scenes "really real" world, for the simple reason that there is no such behind-the-scenes world. The action is right here, and we are the key players in it. In such a view of our human reality, where do guardian angels fit? I would like to suggest that we humans are meant to be guardian angels to one another, a role that has for centuries been largely unappreciated but is now being revived.

Spiritual Separated from Bodily
It is a long and complex story, but very early on in the history of the Mediterranean cultures that are our roots, there emerged a negative attitude toward everything that was material or bodily, with special suspicion being directed to our human bodiliness and sexuality. Rightly, this way of thinking saw the value of the spiritual side of our being, but "spiritual" was separated off from and opposed to "bodily." Achieving the genuinely good life, becoming authentically human, was more and more

equated with denial of the body. Consequently, what was immediately observable because it was material and bodily could not
be the truly worthwhile aspect of our human life; beneath these
observable appearances lay the world of spirit, which, at least to
some extent, was hidden and blocked by matter and body.

Following such a downgrading of bodiliness was the conclusion that "ordinary" human life, life as it is lived by most people,
was definitely second-rate. When this began to affect the understanding of Christian faith and life, the form it took was that "real"
Christianity demanded a removal from bodiliness as far as that
could be achieved. Ordinary family life, which had been
Christianity's first model for the church, obviously involved a
good deal of bodiliness, indeed depended on it for the family's
very existence. So, it was abandoned as the model in favor of the
kind of self-denying life one associates with early monks of the
desert. The real Christian was the spiritual athlete who could exist
with very little attention to the body and so devote full attention
to spiritual things.

This attitude soon linked up with two others: 1) Within a short
time, the early Christian understanding that all the baptized are
called to active participation in the ministries of the church gave
way to the idea that active ministry was meant to be restricted to
those Christians who were special because of their ordination.
Ordinary Christians were more and more reduced to "being
saved" rather than helping to save others. The saving presence of
God was then believed to reside in the ministry of the Holy
Orders, i.e,. the ordained; they and their actions were the sacrament of God's presence. 2) All this crystallized in the basic cultural image of a ladder, with humans arranged in ascending order
with the more spiritual ones, like bishops, being at the top and
closer to God who was pure spirit and material things, including
ordinary and very bodily humans, at the bottom. And, of course,
in this ladder image, the not-quite-complete spirituality of bishops, etc., had to be complemented by pure-spirit angels before
the ladder could reach all the way to God.

Second-Class Status in the Church

So, for centuries, non-ordained Christians were relegated to second-class status in the life of the Church. The notion of "vocation" to active discipleship was limited to those who went on to priestly ordination or entered religious life. Growth in Christian holiness was envisaged in terms of the human spirit becoming ever freer from bodiliness. A favorite title for treatises on Christian "spirituality" was some variant of "the ascent of the mind to God." And Christian art pictured the human soul being freed from the body at death and rising up to heaven.

With such emphasis on downgrading the bodily, the immediately observable, the day-by-day aspects of humans' lives, it is not surprising to find that the routine activities, even the not-so-routine actions of ordinary people were not seen as the context for God's saving presence.

While there were some official church statements about the importance of the family, even some about the dignity of work, if one wished to come into contact with God, it was assumed that this had to take place in the sacred precincts of the church building. Despite St. Paul's insistence that it is the people of faith who are the temple in which God's Spirit dwells, Christians for most of church history have built buildings that they called "the house of God," with the implication that these buildings were the primary place for encountering God.

Today a number of things, not least a more careful reading of the scriptures, have challenged this anti-body confining of God's presence to officially designated persons and places.

A much healthier appreciation of human bodiliness, most notably of human sexuality, has come into the picture. Even the spiritual dimension of humans is now seen to be inextricably bound up with bodiliness. There is no denying that women and men are essentially spiritual beings, all women and men, but they are *embodied* spirits and the very nature of their spirituality is conditioned by this embodiment. "Wellness" is increasingly thought of as embracing bodily health and psychic integrity, with each conditioning the other.

Appreciating the Ordinary

Along with this has come in religious circles, very slowly it is true, a greater appreciation of the "ordinary" and the unofficial. For Catholics a breakthrough statement of this came with Vatican II's recognition that the church is the entire people of God, that discipleship and ministry are the right and the responsibility of all the baptized, and that faith is meant to be expressed and developed by people's involvement with family, jobs, public life, and work for justice and peace. This is reinforced by the Council's document on the liturgy, which insists that all of those gathered for the Eucharist are meant to be active participants. Guided by these insights, theologians in the past quarter century have moved quickly to clarify the basic sacramentality of human life and the special sacramentality of Christians' lives.

This recognition that the Christian church is meant to be a discipleship of equals has been most gratifying for the non-ordained who, at least in theory, are no longer considered "second best." However, it has brought with it the implication that a basic responsibility rests on all the baptized, the responsibility for the human well-being of all their human brothers and sisters, for their physical well-being and their spiritual well-being. Each person in her or his specific life situation is meant, through their diverse ministries to the needs of people, to be a "word" that tells God's compassionate care for people. But more than just a "word" about a compassionate God. They are to be sacrament; in their ministries God's own compassion is present to heal and transform. One could say that humans are meant to be angels to one another; but the reality goes beyond that. It is not just that they are "stand-ins" for God, God's legates in taking care of one another. Instead, their ministry to one another is actually God's ministry as well; their care and concern embody God's. If one uses the term carefully, one can say that their ministry "incarnates" God's saving power, God's own Spirit. That is precisely why Christian ministry is a sacrament.

To a considerable extent this understanding of the caring ministry of all the baptized was obscured; and in its place the

belief in ministering angels came to prominence. The more
guardian angels took over in people's beliefs, the less people
reflected on ministry as a prerogative and responsibility of all
Christians. Thus, there is a danger again today that over-emphasis on angelic presences and angelic ministrations will keep
many Christians from realizing and accepting their own active
discipleship. That, briefly, is why it seems to me that the question of angels' guardianship of humans is not the relevant or
important issue.

Community with Heavenly Friends

Does that mean that there are no guardian angels? Not necessarily. It could well be that in addition to one another, we
humans need the extra help of and to be in community with
"heavenly" friends. Certainly, we should not try to wrench away
from people a devotion that has genuinely brought them closer to
God, authentically reflected the compassion of God, and given
them a sense of security. We would be better advised to follow
the guidance of Vatican II's *Constitution on the Sacred Liturgy*. It
is clear in this document that a positive effort should be made to
move Catholics from a devotional spirituality to a spirituality
bound up with active eucharistic participation.

But the document also indicates that the focus should be a
positive one of fostering this eucharistic activity rather than a negative one of taking away devotions that are dear to people. To the
extent that eucharistic spirituality grows, it will replace the other,
and this is already happening. So, too, with belief in and devotion
to guardian angels: What is important is that Christians discover
the saving presence of God in their own ministry of care for their
sisters and brothers; this discovery may well make guardian
angels a purely abstract question.

What about the faithful
who have gone before us?
If they are with Christ, and share this new life
he won in his living and dying, do they not also
share his continuing activity of salvation?

Chapter Five

WE ARE A COMMUNION OF SAINTS

When the astronauts landed on the moon in 1969, they didn't find any angels there to greet them. But I wonder if their adventure there did not do a lot to increase people's fascination with angels. Standing there on the moon they looked down to earth and saw it as that beautiful blue marble freely floating in the immensity of space, and that picture—since reproduced thousands of times—has helped create an indefinable sense of aloneness among all of us.

Though we might have known theoretically that our Earth is but one relatively small planet in a solar system that is one among millions in the heavens, it was that picture of Earth floating in space, without visible connection to anything, that brought home to us how alone and tiny we really are, scarcely noticeable in the vastness of space. It would have been consoling to know that others like ourselves inhabited other worlds "out there"; that we had neighbors somewhere in the universe. But so far, despite the sophistication of our scientific listening technology, we have not received any messages from outer space—though flying saucer buffs assure us that we have already been visited and will soon make more evident contact with extra-terrestrial voyagers.

In the meantime—and that may be a very long time—we do have the angels to keep us company, in our imaginations if not in reality. The companionship of angels is not, of course, something that entered the picture only with the landing on the moon. For centuries humans have thought of angelic beings as living in the heavens, in some cases responsible for moving the stars and planets. One needs only to read the *Paradiso* of Dante to envisage the grandeur of the heavens filled with the glory of choirs of angels, arrayed in ascending power until they reach the seraphim who surround the throne of the Most High.

Angels Were in Charge

During the centuries of Christianity when the astronomy of Ptolemy was still accepted, and when the influence of Aristotle's explanations of the heavenly bodies and their relation to the earth was unchallenged, angels were believed to be in charge of the stars and planets, moving them in their appointed places. In a subtle way this guaranteed the regularity of nature, for not only did this mean that the heavenly bodies were in good hands, but since these heavenly bodies influenced happenings on our earth, the regular operation of nature could be depended upon.

Angels were not only the guardians of individual humans or of communities of people; they were the guardians of the entire universe. Despite these worldly tasks, the angels' dwelling place was heaven; they were waiting for us to join them and behind the scenes working to assure our final homecoming. They were friends, fellow worshipers of God, already enjoying that unending bliss which is our destiny too. At funerals it was consoling, and still is, to end the liturgy with the beautiful song, "May the angels lead you into paradise." It was consoling, too, to believe that despite their majesty and grandeur we humans could boast of a limited equality or even superiority. Was not the human Jesus the Lord even of the angels and his mother the Queen of the Angels?

So, would it not be a sad loss if there were no such angelic companions on our life's journey, if we really were floating in the vastness of space all by ourselves? Surely, something treasured would be lost; but perhaps something even more consoling exists to take over the role played by the angels in our beliefs and imaginings. That something "new" is what the Christian creeds refer to as "the communion of saints."

Challenging Favored Beliefs

Before we go on to suggest that the communion of saints may have better credentials than guardian angels, it might be good to deal with an objection that is often raised as we take a more critical look at our "traditional" beliefs. Are we not going to lose much of the warm devotional side of our faith if we continue this business of challenging our favorite beliefs? Why bother people with the questions raised by historians and theologians? What harm does it do to leave people to believe in angels if they wish, especially when depriving them of guardian angels may diminish their personal faith?

The question is real; and we have raised it a number of times in the past few decades as critical scholarship was applied to the bible, to official statements of the church, or to our liturgical practice. But in each case, the open-ended and honest search for the truth—for example, about the authorship of the biblical texts— has led us to a deepened insight into God and God's dealings with humans and a richer appreciation for things like the bible. As for raising questions about angels, we already saw in the previous chapter that the positive gain may well come in greater realization of our human dignity and further implementation of our essential role in God's work of salvation.

Belief in a communion of saints is not new. The fact that the early Christian professions of faith explicitly mention it makes that clear. In the very poetry and art that for centuries depicted the angelic choirs, heaven was also peopled with "the saints," those humans whose fidelity to God in their earthly life led to their unending share in angelic joy. When early Christians gathered for sacramental liturgy, they had a sense of sharing in a worship of

God that was being celebrated jointly by themselves and by the Christians who had passed into glory. They felt that they truly were the earthly part of the communion of saints praising God.

However, this felt presence of the saints slowly faded, even though belief in the passage of good people into heaven remained. But old beliefs long dimmed can sometimes become "new" with their rediscovery, which is the case with Christian belief in "the communion of saints." However, more than rediscovery of belief has occurred in recent decades. Based on our more accurate understanding of what is involved in the "resurrection" of Jesus himself, we are now on the brink of discovering more fully what the communion of saints is all about.

Belief in the Afterlife

Exactly what Christians have thought about heaven, hell, and associated topics has never been too clear. Belief that there is an afterlife has remained quite constant as has the idea that our behavior on earth will affect that afterlife, with either blessing or punishment. But what is "heaven" really like? What is the reality of "the beatific vision"? What sort of bodiliness will we possess, a question that was inescapable because of the credal statement that we believe in the "resurrection of the body and life everlasting"? What is "eternal rest" all about; does it suggest that with death we will simply fall asleep and wake up at the end of the world?

One thing has continued over the centuries and tells us that some awareness of linkage between heaven and earth remains. This is people's devotion to their favorite saints. Some, at least of those who have died, are thought to be powerful intercessors with God and at the same time interested in their devotees on earth; so Christians pray to them, make pilgrimages to their burial places, and honor them as outstanding Christian heroes and exemplars. The historical evolution of the annual succession of liturgical feasts emerged from just this devotion to saints.

Overall, I think it would be safe to say that our beliefs in life beyond death are still vague at best, though for centuries the idea has persisted that heaven is somewhere "up there," and Christian art reflects this understanding. We trust that wherever heaven is, our loved ones at death pass over to enjoyment of that unending happiness, and we hope that with our own death we will join them, never again to be separated.

Without questioning the words and images we are using too much, Christians have believed for centuries that heaven is the place to which Jesus ascended soon after his resurrection on Easter. And they took for granted that that was what the gospels were talking about when they witnessed to Jesus' passage into another life. With the help of today's more careful methods of studying the scriptures, we now know that "heaven," "going up to heaven," and "sitting at the right hand of God" are metaphors that the early Christians, and specifically the authors of the gospels, used to express their belief that the Jesus they had known, and whose death had temporarily shattered all their dreams, had passed through death into a new and much superior way of life.

The character of this new life remains even for us today a mystery, and it is expressed by Paul in a letter to the early Christians that "eye has not seen, nor has ear heard, nor has it entered into the human mind what things have been prepared for those who love God." When things exceed our images, ideas, and language, we need to resort to metaphors and this is what we have done in picturing the life beyond as "heaven."

It might be good to state very clearly that this "new" view does not deny that Jesus "rose from the dead." It means that he passed into a different and better state of human life. In this new life he did not go some place apart from our earth, for the simple reason that in that new way of risen life there is no space or time, and therefore no "place" to go. Instead, the risen Jesus remains present to those on this earth who accept his resurrection in faith. This means that throughout human history, the risen Christ remains in immediate contact with the faith-full, present to them in their lives and especially present when they gather together, as they do in Eucharist, "in his name." That is, of course, the way in which Matthew's gospel reports Jesus' last words: "Behold, I am with you all days, even to the end of the world."

Understanding Jesus' resurrection in this way—that he has not gone away from our world but instead remains forever present to us—throws new light on the mystery we have already referred to with the words "communion of saints." What it suggests, and more than suggests, is that those who have passed through death, faithful to themselves as persons and therefore to God, have emerged into a new life in union with the risen Christ. Moreover, these "saints" have not gone any place apart from us. Instead, if they are now united to the risen Christ, and he is constantly present to us, so are they. They still remain united to us in one community of believers in Jesus, the Christ.

Bonds Between Living and Dead

Searching for immortality, somehow conquering the ultimate physical evil of death and its threat to the very meaning of human existence, has preoccupied humans as far as we can trace human history. Ancient stories, like that of Gilgamesh from ancient Mesopotamia, or that of Adam and Eve in Israel's traditions, try to explain why it is that humans do not have the answer to death, its origin, or the means to overcome it. At the same time, there has been a consistent belief in many cultures that some link remains between the living and the dead. In some cases this has been a reverent respect for ancestors, in others, a fear that the dead will haunt those who in life had injured them. Still today, in Hispanic cultures the *Dia de los muertos* is an occasion for people to gather in cemeteries and spend some time in communion with the loved ones who have died. And in many places in Europe, church attendance swells on Palm Sunday as Christians come to obtain the palms which they then lay on the graves of the deceased as signs of belief in risen life.

Many people worldwide have some sense that the dead are not totally out of contact with the living. In some cultures, particularly in Africa, this link of living and dead is particularly prominent and colors the everyday lives of people. Those familiar with contemporary Afro-American literature know how frequently the characters in this writing pass easily back and forth from one world to another, from the world of the living to dealing with the dead. We can't but wonder what will happen when in the very near future the rapidly growing numbers of African Christians will influence the thinking of the church. It seems to me that this African consciousness of communing with those who have gone before us will begin to open up and intensify the Christian belief in a communion of saints.

No matter what future developments are, the notion of communication between the Christian community of this world and the community of "the saved" in the life beyond death will remain part of Christian belief. As such, it is a reassurance that we are not alone in the universe, that "home" is a reality that lies before us, that dying is not so much a loss as it is a gain, for it will be our true "homecoming" when we will be welcomed into the everlasting community of those who allowed God to save them.

Christ Is Still Active

There is another aspect of Jesus' risen state that throws light on the communion of saints—or at least tantalizes our imaginings about the next life. For long we thought that with his passage into risen life, Jesus had completed his mission in history and had passed on his ministry to those who generation by generation succeeded him in this world. Careful reading on and reflection about the New Testament and the beliefs that underlie it have changed this view. Jesus as the risen Christ did not cease from ministry. Instead, endowed now with the full power of God's Spirit, Christ has entered upon a much more active phase of his ministry. Whereas before it was limited to a few short years and to the relatively small area of Galilee and Judaea, Christ's work of healing human life now knows no limits of space or time. It stretches throughout the world and throughout human history.

What about the faithful who have gone before us? If they are with Christ, and share this new life he won in his living and dying, do they not also share his continuing activity of salvation? The very heart of all Christian ministry is the love and care we have

for our human sisters and brothers. Clearly, those who (with us)
form one communion of saints, have not ceased to love. Indeed,
we have always believed that the imperfect love they (and we)
have in this life will come to full expression in the life beyond
death. What this seems to say to me is that those who have died
with faith remain part of the ultimate human story that is God's
history. They are part of God's reign of truth and love as generation after generation of women and men are drawn to their destiny by the power of God's inviting Spirit.

If we have the risen Christ
and if his Abba is always present to us
in their Spirit, where do angels fit in?
Do we really need them?

Chapter Six

LINGERING QUESTIONS
ABOUT ANGELS

S everal of my friends and editors
were good enough to supply me with questions that came to
them after reading the first draft of this book. They provide a view
of the questions readers may have and some of them present a
serious challenge to my view of angels; so, it would be less than
honest not to take account of them. At the very beginning, however, I would like to stress that my purpose has not been to make
a firm claim about the non-existence of angels; it is just that I see
no need for them and fear that concentrating on them may pre-
vent us from appreciating the saving presence of the risen Christ.

Probably the most serious objection comes from the centuries-
long devotion of Christians to their guardian angel or to Michael
the archangel. Was their devotion and prayer directed to a non-
existent reality? I don't believe so, even if there are no angels. The
very heart of that long-standing devotion was the trust they had

in a guarding and caring God. Since in their imaginations they placed God at a distance, up in heaven, angels were seen as the messengers of God, God's legates for carrying on the divine saving work in the world. People were mistaken to the extent that they imaged God as being distant, a mistake that has been gradually corrected over past centuries as we recovered the awareness of God's abiding presence to us, but people were not mistaken in their belief about God's compassionate care.

Should Belief in Angels Be Discouraged?

Another questioner raised a very practical question: Should we try to argue people out of their belief in angels and encourage them to stop praying to their guardian angel? It seems to me that the answer to this lies in the approach taken toward devotional practices in Vatican II's *Constitution on the Sacred Liturgy*. The document leaves no doubt that the council is directing Catholics to make the celebration of Eucharist once again the center and model of their prayer. This implies that we need to move away from the over-emphasis on various devotions that for long had obscured the centrality of eucharistic worship. But in the latter portion of this document, the council insists that people should not be forced to give up the devotions that have brought them closer to God. It also says, however, that increased involvement with eucharistic worship can deepen people's faith, prayer, and sense of closeness to God and diminish their need for and attachment to the devotional practices that had once nourished their faith. The council did not deny that devotions are good, but insisted that something else is better. So, too, it seems to me that devotion to a guardian angel is good but a growing awareness of the abiding presence of God in Christ and the Spirit is better.

I think the incident I related in chapter two (the one in which the noted scripture scholar, though he found no convincing evidence for angels in the bible, still continued the practice of praying to his guardian angel), says something important to this question. When he said "I pray to mine [his guardian angel] every day," he was fully conscious that at the heart of this practice is his deep trust in God's loving providence. If devotion to a guardian angel makes people more aware of and more appreciative of God's saving care, then there is no good reason for encouraging them to change—unless this stands in the way of their becoming more aware of and appreciative of God's presence to them in and through the presence of the risen Christ.

What Should We Teach?

A related question: What does one do, then, catechetically? Should we continue to tell children about their guardian angel, even if we are uncertain about the existence of that heavenly helper? Personally, I would concentrate on the abiding presence of the risen Christ. It seems to me that an awareness of this constant divine help and protection would provide at least as much of a sense of security as devotion to a guardian angel. Moreover, I believe that at some later date this awareness of Christ's presence, if it has been developed, could help them appreciate the mystery of the communion of saints. On the other hand, I know that some imaginative and sensitive teachers of the young do incorporate angels into their catechesis. Just this past summer, one of my students in a master's-level course on Christology created (in lieu of a standard term paper) a creative instructional video in which guardian angels played a prominent role.

A particular catechetical problem arises because of the mention of angels in the eucharistic liturgy, especially at the moment when we are invited to join them in singing "Holy, holy, holy...." Behind such liturgical mention of angels lies the notion, centuries old, that there is one cosmic praise of God, one liturgy, in which Christians on earth join with the heavenly hosts in praising God. Our liturgical prayer reflects this: We are only the earthly part of the unending worship of God. Again, however, the imagery connected with such prayer is really part of our attempt in metaphor to attain some idea of what union with God in the next life is all about. Since God is ruler of the universe, triumphant over evil and the majestic Lord of all, how would we not imagine his royal court to be filled with courtiers like angels? So, why not explain such mention of heaven and angels as metaphors, and insist that the wondrous reality of God defies our attempts to attain some adequate understanding? Why not let God be God—beyond our images or ideas?

Why Emphasize Saints and Not Angels?

Two of the questioners who raised this issue of catechetical instruction regarding angels linked saints with angels: How would you explain the place of angels and saints to children in a religion class? It seems to me that angels and saints are two different matters. Saints are those faithful humans who after their death pass into union with the risen Christ and enjoy the fulfillment of human existence that we all hope to share.

As I tried to explain in chapter five, these faithful departed whom we remember in the eucharistic prayer of the liturgy are not off in some distant heaven but are still present to us. With them we form one body of Christ, one communion of saints, something that has been mentioned in the Christian creeds from the beginning. For us they not only are brothers and sisters in the family of faith, they (and especially those whose Christian life was markedly faith-filled) serve as models of what it means to be Christian. Since these Christian brothers and sisters of ours—who have already conquered death and are living in union with the risen Christ—are part of the community of believers to which we belong, we can depend on their interest and concern for us, and there is no reason why we should not on occasion turn to them in prayer. We seek help from one another here on earth as we try to come closer to God; why should we not do the same with the saints? The church's teaching about the communion of saints is quite different from what is said, or not said, about angels.

What Does the Church Teach?

What, then, is the official teaching of the church about angels? Angels, not explicitly guardian angels, are clearly mentioned, for example, in the prayers of the eucharistic liturgy. But we must ask whether they are mentioned as something *assumed* in the overall cultural view of Christians at the time the statement was made. Perhaps the most doctrinally important statement was made by the Fourth Council of the Lateran (in 1215) when it talks about the creation of both material and spiritual beings. However, as one reads this text carefully, it is clear that the intent of the council is not to confirm the existence of angels but to deny the existence of spiritual beings (like angels) who are not created by God. This teaching of the council was directed quite clearly against the Manichean teaching that in addition to the world created by God there was another parallel and opposed world of powerful spirits. So, as far as I can see and have been able to discover by study, the existence of angels, including guardian angels, is not a matter of required faith; one can be a good believing Christian whether believing in angels or not.

Are There Really Choirs of Angels?

But if this is true, if angels are only incidental to faith and perhaps do not even exist, why has the church passed on a listing of the nine choirs of angels, seraphim and cherubim, etc., and where did this listing come from? The precise origin of it is not clear, but one of the earliest—if not the earliest—list came from a writing of Pseudo-Dionysius the Areopagite. Though this sixth-century Christian theologian identified himself as "Dionysius the Areopagite," that was not really his name. The real Dionysius was the convert of St. Paul, made as a result of Paul's preaching in Athens. By using this name, Pseudo-Dionysius was read as if he were a direct witness to the teachings of Paul.

What added extra plausibility to his list was Paul's mention of powerful spirits like "principalities and powers"; however, this mention comes in the Pauline letter to the Colossians where the "principalities and powers" referred to are not what Christians would call angels. Rather, they are the mysterious powers believed in by Gnosticism, a belief Paul is warning Christians not to share. Notions about more-than-earthly powers were widespread in the Mediterranean world during the early centuries of Christianity; the Hebrew Bible—taken over by Christianity—mentions seraphs and cherubs as part of God's heavenly court; and (as I mentioned in chapter two) the later strata of the bible, particularly the book of Daniel, talk of angels and even archangels like Michael. And, of course, that highly symbolic writing, the book of Revelation, is filled with angels of various kinds. Gradually all this came together in Pseudo-Dionysius' writing, *The Celestial Hierarchy,* and because of his supposed credentials was accepted as Christian belief. This somewhat dubious origin does not prove that there is no such hierarchy of angels. Pseudo-Dionysius may have been merely reflecting what was common teaching in his time. But there is no independent evidence of this and there is some indication that the neat nine-level arrangement of angels was his imaginative creation.

Why Did Jesus Refer To Angels?

However, another question posed to me seems to cut deeper: "What did Jesus mean when he referred to angels; what would his image have been as a person living in that time?" First of all, it seems rather striking that angels seem to play only a very incidental part in Jesus' own parables which are the heart of his teaching. There are only four passages in which the Greek word "aggelos" (which itself means simply "a messenger") occurs in Jesus' speech. There is one occurrence in Luke's account of the parable of the shepherd who seeks the lost sheep which mentions that "there is more joy among the angels in heaven...." This seems simply to pick up the assumed religious metaphor of God's heavenly court that was current during centuries of Judaism and which as a Jew of his day Jesus probably shared. I don't know what Jesus would have responded if he had been asked: "Do you think there really is such a multitude of angelic beings who surround the throne of God?" Incidentally, when John's gospel mentions the "good shepherd," there is no reference to angels.

In another text, this time in Matthew's account of Jesus' arrest in Gethsemane, Jesus says to one of his disciples that he (Jesus) could call upon God for twelve legions of angels, i.e., a heavenly army. While these words of Jesus certainly fit well into the account, it is difficult to establish that we are here dealing with words Jesus actually used on that occasion. The parallel passages in the other two synoptics make no mention of angels. What the passage does reflect is the "heavenly hosts" were probably taken for granted by Christians, indeed by the entire Jewish Hellenistic culture, at the time the gospel was written. Other mentions of angels in the gospels have to do with the final judgment (Mt 13:39, 16:27, 24:31; Mk 8:38) or with the scenes of the empty tomb (Mt 28:2–6). In general, the mention of angels in the bible is part of the image of God's heavenly court where God is surrounded by angelic courtiers or warriors. It is good to bear in mind that God's heavenly court is a metaphor.

What Should Homilists Preach?

It is not only catechists who are faced with the question of how to deal with the mention of angels in the bible or the liturgy. As one of my questioners mentioned, homilists face a special challenge at Christmas and Easter when angels figure prominently in some of the liturgical readings. I think there is an answer to this problem, but it is complicated and depends on the methods for reading the bible accurately. Very briefly, both the infancy narratives describing Jesus' birth and the accounts of Jesus' resurrection are special forms of literature that cannot be treated as if they were simply factual descriptions of something that happened. Something did happen, something of unparalleled importance, but something beyond the power of ordinary language to convey; so, story and metaphor are used. This means, however, that we cannot argue from the text to establish the actuality of details in the account.

The passage that seems closest to Jesus' own view of guardian angels (actually the only gospel reference to *guardian* angels) is in Mt 18:10. In that scene Jesus says that "the little ones" are not to be despised, for "their angels are constantly in the presence of God in heaven." Even in this text it is not clear that one is speaking of angels who accompany humans to guide and guard them, for it speaks of "their angels" as being in heaven.

What about Angelic "Experiences"?

Several of the questions posed to me dealt with people's reports that they had actually experienced angels. These reports I take quite seriously and at least in some cases they seem to be based on very genuine experiences. One of the most striking was the case (reported in the press) of a little girl at the moment of death crying out to her mother, "Mother I see the angels coming to greet me." I can quite easily accept the reality of her experience. So, doesn't that argue for the reality of angels? My response: Not necessarily. How would I defend this response?

Such experiences, even those that are genuine—and many instead are psychological projections of one sort or another—are tricky to analyze. Clearly, there is some input from the person's previous understandings, imaginings, etc., that enter into the interpretation that is part of every human experience. In the case of the dying child, even though the experience of being welcomed into the next life may very well have been "objective" and not the product of the child's expectations, one has to ask where the element of *seeing* comes in, because angels are by definition invisible. It seems to me that one also has to ask why the "welcomers" are identified as angels; at least to some extent this must have come from previous catechizing about heaven being the dwelling place of angels. If there were persons there to welcome the child, why could it not just as well have been some of the faithful departed humans with whom the child had already been linked in the communion of saints?

Let me just mention as another piece of my response an experience of a person whom I know quite well and whose account of the experience leaves no doubt in my mind. That individual was at the bedside of his mother as she was dying and he saw his father, who had been dead for more than twenty years, coming to welcome her into risen life. As he reports the experience, the "seeing" was not exactly the kind of vision we regularly enjoy, but it was a seeing in which his father was immediately recognizable even though in appearance he looked as he had as a young man.

Personally, I have no good reason for questioning the reality of what happened in this case, though I certainly cannot explain it. I do believe, however, that it is quite compatible with what we have come to believe about the "communion of saints." Does that say that the dying child's experience could not have come from angels actually coming to welcome her? Not at all, but it suggests to me that much of what is attributed to angels may actually belong to the "saints," i.e., the faithful who already enjoy risen life.

Are There Really "Fallen Angels"?

Finally, a number of the questions had to do with "fallen angels." Are there really such, and if so what is their role? One questioner asked why God did not simply get rid of the "bad angels." Why didn't God just destroy Lucifer and his minions instead of casting them down into hell for eternal punishment? Underlying all these questions is the basic one: Are there "bad angels"; is the devil a reality? If there are no such beings, we obviously don't have to be concerned about God's treatment of them. If there are "bad angels," we don't know why God has allowed them to exist and cause problems for humans—what we do know in faith is that God's help is more than sufficient for us to deal with these tempters.

I've never found a convincing argument one way or the other regarding the existence of the "devil," though I must confess to being rather skeptical. Without a doubt, some of the "evidence" that people point to as confirmation of the devil's existence, especially the phenomena surrounding what are considered diabolical possessions, is striking. But there is very little of this, perhaps none of it, that cannot find an alternative explanation in terms of such things as very deep psychosis.

As for the biblical mention of Lucifer, Satan, the devil, and such, the arguments for the actual existence of evil spirits is weakened by two things: 1) Belief in such evil forces was a taken-for-granted element of popular understanding of the world at the time the biblical literature was written, and so cannot be seen as something especially revealed by God; and 2) Practically all of the texts that speak about Lucifer battling with Michael, being cast down into hell, etc. (Rv. 12, for example), are to be found in books written in the highly symbolic style of the apocalyptic literature where the statements are obviously not to be taken at face value. In short, I just don't know for certain, but I have serious doubts.

So, I end where I began: If we have the risen Christ and his Abba always present to us in their Spirit, if we are "words" for one another, sacraments by which God is made present to us, and if we are accompanied in our joys and sorrows, our achievements and our frailty, by the host of those friends who now live unendingly beyond death, where do angels fit in? Do we really need them?

CONTINUING THE DISCUSSION

We encourage you to discuss *Why Angels?* with other members of small groups. These questions will get you started.

Chapter One

•Cooke writes: "Faced with the loss of 'spirit' in our materialistic society, we cling to the notion that there is a world of spirits who, though superior to us, are still involved with us and somehow are part of our world." Do you agree or disagree with this statement?

•What about this statement: "Perhaps the prominence of angels is a forecast of God's intensified presence to our history; perhaps before we humans can admit the awesome reality of divine presence, we have to prepare for it by rumors of angels." Do you agree or disagree?

•Cooke says that the term "the angel of the Lord" refers to God's own appearances to privileged humans, and not to some creatures other than God. What do you make of this?

•Do you think that most people are aware of God's presence? Why or why not? Do you think that most people believe in angels?

•Jesus said, "Behold I am with you all days, even to the end of the world." Why would we need guardian angels if we have Jesus' own guarding care?

Chapter Two
•What does the mystery of "God's Presence" mean to you? How would you explain it to one of your children, to a co-worker, to a close friend?

•Do you believe that God is involved with you on a personal, daily basis? Why or why not?

•Cooke says: "If there are angelic guardians protecting and guiding us, they would truly be a 'word' about the God who lovingly cares for us." What do you think he means?

•If Jesus is "the sacrament of the presence of God," what part would angels play in our spiritual lives?

•Cooke asks: "Why are angels so popular today? I wonder if it is because people for the most part have not discovered the reality of divine presence." What is your reaction to this statement? Would it be true of you and those close to you?

Chapter Three
•Commenting on the present interest in angels, Cooke writes: "Power far beyond the human surrounds us and is at our disposal, but it is not the power reflected in a psychic fair." Do you agree or disagree? What power might he mean?

•Cooke says: "The power that is meaningful for me and that makes all the other claims to spirit-power weak and irrelevant is what Christian faith calls the Holy Spirit." Have you ever experienced the Holy Spirit as "power" in your life?

•"God's Spirit is life-giving in the deepest sense because this Spirit *is* God's self-giving love. But what can this mean to us humans who still live with such a different notion of 'power'?" How would you answer this question?

•How would you answer if asked, "Who is the Holy Spirit?" How would you answer, "Who are angels?" Cooke maintains that because we have the power of the Holy Spirit, we do not need powerful angels. How do you feel about this?

•If we believe that God is present through the Holy Spirit, what purpose would angels have in our lives? Is it a question of "either/or"? Can we believe in both? Why or why not?

Chapter Four

•Cooke asks: "Couldn't we just take or leave angels? Wouldn't life and even one's relation to God go on just about the same with or without angels?" How would you answer?

•"God's presence is not something that comes and goes except in so far as we are more or less conscious of it. God's self-gift to us in presence is a great mystery, but that does not mean that it is hidden." In what ways do you experience God's presence? Is this a personal reality for you or an abstract one? Explain why.

•Cooke writes: "There are no unimportant people, there is no 'secular' world that is not touched and made sacred by God's presence, though there can be sinful elements in the world that result from purposeful rejection of this presence." St. Paul says it this way: "If God is for us, who can be against?" What part would angels play in light of these statements?

•"Each person in her or his specific life situation is meant, through their diverse ministries to the needs of people, to be a 'word' that tells of God's compassionate care for people." Have you ever thought of yourself as a "word" that reveals God's love and care? Are you willing to be such a "word"?

•"What is important is that Christians discover the saving presence of God in their own ministry of care for their sisters and brothers. This discovery may well make guardian angels a purely abstract question." How do you react to this statement?

Chapter Five

•"For centuries humans have thought of angelic beings as living in the heavens, arrayed in ascending power until they reach the seraphim who surround the throne of the Most High." Is this your image? Why or why not?

•"Would it not be a sad loss if there were no such angelic companions on our life's journey, if we really were floating in the vastness of space all by ourselves? Surely something treasured would be lost; but perhaps something even more consoling exists to take over the role played by angels in our beliefs and imaginings." To what do you think Cooke is referring here? What is the "something even more consoling"?

•What do you understand the term "communion of saints" to mean? Do you feel part of such a communion? In what ways?

•"The risen Christ remains in immediate contact with the faith-full, present to them in their lives and especially present when they gather together as they do in Eucharist, 'in his name.'" What does this statement mean for you? In what ways do you experience this presence?

•Cooke asks: "What about the faithful who have gone before us? If they are with Christ, and share this new life he won in his living and dying, do they not also share his continuing activity of salvation?" Have you ever considered the role of those you love who have died? Have you thought of them as continuing the activity of salvation, perhaps on your behalf?

Chapter Six
•Do you believe in guardian angels? Why or why not? How would you articulate your belief?
•Should you encourage children to pray to angels? How would you explain their place in the Christian story?

•What does the church teach about angels? Where might you find more about this?

•Do you believe that there are choirs of angels? Where did this "ranking" originate and why would it be important? What do you think St. Paul meant when he referred to "principalities and powers"?

•If there are no angels (or if they are not essential to our faith), why would Jesus have referred to them?

•What are we to think of people who claim to have had angelic "experiences"? How do you feel about these experiences?

•Cooke says: "If we have the risen Christ and his Abba always present to us in their Spirit, where do angels fit in?" How would you answer?

Of Related Interest...

Sacraments & Sacramentality
Bernard Cooke
Explores the mysteries of redemption, church, human life, and love all in relationship to sacraments and sacramentality.
588-7, 250 pp, $14.95 (order code B-85)

The Creed (revised edition)
Berard L. Marthaler
Links the present to the past by drawing on recent biblical scholarship, liturgical studies, theological explanations and historical research.
537-2, 456 pp, $19.95 (order code B-75)

Catholic Customs and Traditions
A Popular Guide
Greg Dues
How did the rosary originate? What meaning do certain colors have in our worship? Why are oils important? These and other curiosities are explained in this revised and expanded edition.
515-1, 224 pp, $9.95 (order code C-14)

Pilgrim Church
A Popular History of Catholic Christianity
William J. Bausch
General readers will enjoy this concise and comprehensive study of the history of Catholic Christianity.
395-7, 480 pp, $12.95 (order code B-52)

Available at religious bookstores or from

XXIII TWENTY-THIRD PUBLICATIONS
P.O. Box 180 • Mystic, CT 06355

To Order or request a free catalog of other quality books and video call:
1-800-321-0411